The New Ranch Handbook:
A Guide to Restoring Western Rangelands

by Nathan F. Sayre

for the Quivira Coalition

The Quivira Coalition
551 Cordova Road, #423
Santa Fe, New Mexico 87501
www.quiviracoalition.org

ISBN # 0-9708264-0-0

Printed in the United States of America

TABLE OF CONTENTS

"Grass is the forgiveness of nature-- her constant benediction....Its tenacious fibers hold the earth in its place, and prevent its soluble components from washing into the wasting sea."

--James Ingalls

The New Ranch Handbook

The New Ranch Handbook

Front Cover

Macho Creek. The effect of dormant season grazing on riparian restoration. [Top] Before dormant season grazing, May 1998; [bottom] after dormant season grazing instituted, September 2000. (Photos courtesy of Courtney White.)

Back Cover

Gray Ranch, 1998. Monitoring as part of an Outdoor Classroom on Rangeland Health sponsored by the Quivira Coalition. (Photo courtesy of Courtney White.)

p. iii: Animal impact on Forest Service land near Cuba, New Mexico. Old corral, where many cows were held prior to shipping, on right. (Photo courtesy of Courtney White.)

p. vi: Fenceline contrast on Sam Montoya's Ranch on Sandia Pueblo, showing how cattle can be used to "knock back" invasive Russian Olive trees. (Photo courtesy of Courtney White.)

p. viii: Tour of Empire Ranch, south of Tucson, Arizona. (Photo courtesy of Courtney White.)

p. 2: Overgrazing on San Carlos Apache Reservation in central Arizona. (Photo courtesy of Kirk Gadzia.)

p. 6: Sid Goodloe, seeding his ranch. (Photo courtesy of Sid Goodloe.)

p. 9: Controlled grazing in Hawaii. (Photo courtesy of Kirk Gadzia.)

p. 19: David and Tammy Ogilvie. (Photo courtesy of Courtney White.)

p. 21: An overburden pile being reclaimed by cattle at a mine site near Cuba, New Mexico. (Photo courtesy of Courtney White.)

p. 33: Mac Donaldson in Cienega Creek riparian area of Empire Ranch. (Photo courtesy of Nathan Sayre.)

p. 35: Beaver dam on Cimarron River, CS Ranch. (Photo courtesy of Courtney White.)

p. 45: Roger Bowe. (Photo courtesy of Roger Bowe.)

p. 48: Kris Havstad on an area of the Jornada Experimental Range which has passed a threshold. (Photo courtesy of USDA.)

p. 59: Jim Winder on his Double Lightning Ranch. (Photo courtesy of Courtney White.)

p. 62: Prescribed fire on Carrizo Valley Ranch. (Photo courtesy of Sid Goodloe.)

p. 75: Jim and Joy Williams. (Photo courtesy of Courtney White.)

p. 77: Kirk Gadzia, Jim Williams, and Steve Libby of the U.S. Forest Service discussing a new grazing plan for the Williams Ranch. (Photo courtesy of Courtney White.)

p. 87: Volunteers from Quail Unlimited constructing fence on Macho Creek. (Photo courtesy of Courtney White.)

p. 92: Prescribed fire on Carrizo Valley Ranch. (Photo courtesy of Sid Goodloe.)

Foreword

by
George B. Ruyle
Professor
and Chair,
Rangeland and
Forest Resources
Program,
The University of
Arizona

The New Ranch Handbook: A Guide to Restoring Western Rangelands promises much in title and delivers more in substance. The book addresses the multitude of contemporary issues facing rangeland management as a profession and ranching as a livelihood. The vision is not just for livestock production but blends environmental concerns with social and cultural values as well. In this regard, Dr. Sayre is not encumbered by the traditional dogma of range managers and yet is able to select the best of that profession's literature and precepts. These include new principles in defoliation effects, an increased understanding of fire, and continued theoretical examination of succession, stability, and range condition. Less documented and highly controversial subjects that affect ranching are not overlooked. Included are such concerns as biodiversity, biological crusts, and endangered species. These are brought together in the context of ranching applications as they never have been before.

Underlying themes include sustainability and the application of science to management. Range livestock grazing is presented as an ecological process, to be judged by management objectives and monitoring. While short duration grazing is clearly discussed, flexible grazing schedules that meet the requirements of each location and manager are emphasized.

The book may serve both as a textbook and as a reference manual. As a textbook, it may be broadly applied to both biological and social sciences. It will also serve as a reference manual for extension, research, and land management agency personnel. As such it blends concepts and principles with their application. For example, the "Ranch Profile" sections are a meticulous portrait of the infinite difficulties, skills, and solutions required to apply science to ranch management.

New insights are revealed that may require grazing managers and scientists to modify present concepts and practices. It is certain that grazing management policies must remain dynamic and flexible in order to accommodate new principles and applications as they become more fully documented. Here you will find a synthesis of the concepts, research data, and application experience necessary to justify the lofty title.

PREFACE

"The art of land doctoring is being practiced with vigor, but the science of land health is yet to be born."
--Aldo Leopold

During the past thirty years, while the debate over public lands grazing has grown increasingly shrill, a small number of people have quietly worked to resolve problems where it counts: on the ground. They have come together at the local level, where their knowledge and concern are greatest, to learn from each other and from the lands they share. Their work has not been fast or easy, and many questions remain to be answered. But they have produced results: ranches where pastures are more productive and diverse, where erosion has diminished, where streams and springs that were dry now flow. Ranches where wildlife are more abundant. Ranches that are more profitable for their owners, even in the highly competitive and difficult business of cattle production.

The Quivira Coalition has coined the term "the New Ranch" to refer to these places. Founded in 1997 by two conservationists and a rancher, Quivira is a non-profit organization dedicated to resolving the so-called "rangeland conflict" through common sense and grassroots collaboration. Central to this goal is spreading the word that ecologically healthy rangeland and economically robust ranches can be compatible. Indeed, the two go hand in hand, because productive land is fundamental to profitable ranching. The natural processes that sustain wildlife habitat, biological diversity, and functioning watersheds are the same processes that make land productive for grazing livestock. The key issue is not whether grazing occurs, but how it is managed. Coalition members have seen this demonstrated on New Ranches in Arizona, New Mexico, and Colorado, and no doubt there are others elsewhere.

The goals of *The New Ranch Handbook* are:

1. To describe management practices that have succeeded in improving both the conservation values and the economic sustainability of a handful of ranches in the arid and semiarid Southwest. The practices described do not add up to any single blueprint or recipe for successful management. Indeed, one of the lessons they teach is that management must be flexible and attentive to the particular circumstances of each ranch's landscape and conditions.

2. To situate these management practices in a framework of scientific research that helps to explain their success. Arid and semiarid rangelands are complex ecosystems, and they defy some of the central ideas of classic ecological theory. Only in the past couple of decades have scientists begun to develop models that account for these unique characteristics. Many details are still poorly or incompletely understood, but several key ecological processes have been scientifically described: the flow of energy, the cycling of water, and the cycling of nutrients. These processes interact to influence the development of communities of plants, animals, soils and humans. They are thus the basis for understanding the science of the New Ranch.

3. To offer a common vocabulary and set of concepts for ranchers, scientists, agency officials, and environmentalists to use in addressing rangeland issues. All these groups share a concern for the land, but all too often they lack a common language to communicate their views and resolve their differences.

4. To increase awareness of the complexity and difficulty of managing rangelands well. No one group—public or private, consumptive or non-consumptive—has a monopoly on good stewardship. Those people who manage land well should be recognized and supported no matter what their backgrounds may be. It is hard work and when done well, it benefits us all.

We have endeavored to achieve these goals in plain language, with a minimum of jargon and abstraction. Where the ideas are complex, they are illustrated with concrete examples. The ideas presented are relevant to rangelands anywhere, but particularly in arid and semiarid regions such as the Southwest and the Great Basin.

A few words about the subtitle. "Restoring Western Rangelands" refers to conserving, restoring, and/or enhancing the basic ecological processes and functions that support rangeland health (see p. 11): soil stability, watershed function, nutrient and energy flows, and resistance and resilience to disturbance. Healthy rangelands, thus defined, are beneficial to wildlife, biological diversity, water quality and quantity, and livestock alike.

Jim Winder
Courtney White
Barbara Johnson
Nathan F. Sayre

Acknowledgements

This book is the product of many people's ideas, experiences, and generosity. I wish to thank first the ranchers who shared their knowledge and helped me to see their lands through their eyes: Roger Bowe, Mac Donaldson, Sid Goodloe, Phil Knight, Mike and Cathy McNeil, David Ogilvie, Virgil Trujillo, Jim Williams, and Jim Winder. Thanks also to their families, who treated me with the warm hospitality that so distinguishes the ranching community.

The original idea for this book belongs to Jim Winder and Dr. Kris Havstad. The Quivira Coalition was born on Jim's ranch—in spirit at least—and Jim's ranch, in turn, reflects many years of dialogue between an innovative rancher and a supremely talented scientist. In many ways, I have simply expanded and formalized their ideas. I can only hope that the pages that follow do justice to the breadth and depth of their knowledge, their commitment, and their contributions to sustainable ranching in the West.

Numerous members and directors of the Quivira Coalition also provided astute comments and helpful guidance: Dan Dagget, Frank Hayes, Dutch Salmon, Kirk Gadzia, Mark McCollum, and Jeff Herrick. George Ruyle, Dan Robinett, Bill McDonald, and Jim Thorpe graciously read and critiqued earlier drafts. My thanks to all.

Thanks also to all who contributed photographs to this handbook: Roger Bowe, Dan Dagget, Kirk Gadzia, Sid Goodloe, Kris Havstad, Cathy McNeil, Phil Ogden, Courtney White, and Jim Winder. And thanks to Carol Roman for the graphic on p. 13.

Finally, to Courtney White and Barbara Johnson, who raised the funds, coordinated the logistics, and served as hosts, photographers, editors, sounding boards, taskmasters, and above all friends: thank you.

Nathan F. Sayre

Substantial funding for production of this *Handbook* was provided by the Thaw Charitable Trust and the National Fish and Wildlife Foundation.

The New Ranch Handbook:
A Guide to Restoring Western Rangelands

Introduction

"Want to know an easy way to make a small fortune? Start with a large one and buy a ranch."
--*Joke among ranchers*

In the frontier period, cattle ranching was widely described as an easy way to make money in the Southwest. Grass was abundant. Springs and streams were available for the taking, if not common. Cattle thrived and reproduced on their own. As one booster put it, a rancher could "sit in the shade of his hacienda, enjoy the good things of life and see his wealth increase on every hill and valley."

At that time, there was no such thing as range science. There were no experts, no textbooks in range management, no handbooks such as this one.

Today, the situation is reversed. Making a living in ranching grows ever more difficult.

Ranchers cannot afford to sit in the shade. If they did, they would see their wealth disappear, not increase. Range management has developed into an entire academic discipline, with its own journals and textbooks and conferences. The amount of technical and scientific information about ranching is so large that making sense of it all could be a full-time job in itself. If early ranchers had too little knowledge of the land, today's ranchers might well feel that they have too much.

Of course this contrast is somewhat exaggerated. Early ranchers faced all kinds of problems, from extremes of weather to disease and isolation. Making money was rarely as simple as the boosters proclaimed it to be. And the problems facing ranching today are not the consequence of too much scientific information—on the contrary, the science has been motivated by the need to solve the problems. But the question remains: what has happened between then and now?

During the first sixty-odd years of cattle ranching in the Southwest, from the 1870s up until the Taylor Grazing Act of 1934, uncontrolled grazing during drought periods resulted in drastic damage to rangelands *[12, 43, 98, 124]*. This was true throughout the West, but it was particularly severe in the Southwestern deserts. Large areas of perennial grassland were reduced to bare soil. Combined with locally severe timber cutting in upland watersheds, accelerated erosion, and increasingly effective fire suppression, the cattle boom precipitated widespread and lasting changes in the region's vegetation *[7]*.

The degradation of the boom period, in turn, prompted the birth of range science. Early range researchers believed that the land would return to its prior condition once cattle numbers were regulated and properly distributed. The fewer the cattle, the more quickly this would occur. As range science grew into an established discipline in the first half of the twentieth century, this belief persisted. Research appeared to confirm it, and the cardinal principles of proper numbers, season of use, and distribution of use became the basis for most

federal range policies. But the seminal research informing this paradigm was conducted in areas with greater or more reliable rainfall than occurs in the arid and semiarid Southwest *[30, 91]*. Southwestern rangelands have improved in the last fifty years or so, but they have not completely returned to their earlier conditions. Often, woody species like mesquite, juniper, and creosote have spread, to the detriment of grasses. This has been documented even in areas excluded from cattle grazing for many decades *[4, 5, 55, 116]*.

After World War II, many ranchers and researchers resorted to expensive programs of brush removal and revegetation to reestablish grasses. These efforts succeeded in restoring some of the lost productivity of Southwestern rangelands, but they are now seen as too expensive to be practiced on a large scale *[34, 89]*. Economic returns per animal are too small. Thirty or forty years ago, some ranchers could afford to invest in chaining, grubbing, and seeding. But today these things are harder to justify on the bottom line. Further improvement will have to come from "natural" sources—that is, by tapping into the capacity of range ecosystems to restore themselves *[46]*.

In one sense, we are back where we began. As in the 1870s, a successful ranch depends on the natural productivity of the range. Healthy economics flow from healthy land. The difference is that today's ranchers have scientific information that yesterday's did not. The scien-

"Southwestern rangelands have improved in the last fifty years or so, but they have not completely returned to their earlier conditions."

An over-rested plant. (Photo courtesy of Kirk Gadzia.)

in the past and points out their shortcomings. These tools fail to apprehend the variability of rangelands across different scales of space and time. Other tools are needed, tools designed to match the underlying ecological processes of arid and semiarid rangelands.

tists still disagree on many of the details, but they have begun to develop explanations and models specific to arid and semiarid rangelands. These models, combined with the concrete examples of good management presented below, form the basis for this handbook.

Before each chapter, there is a brief profile of a ranch where ecological health and economic success have resulted from management practices implemented in the past forty years. In certain details, the profiles illustrate points developed in the chapters they precede. Additional ranches and issues are discussed in boxes throughout the text.

Chapter One asks how ranching can be understood as a form of sustainable agriculture. It examines the tools that have been used to evaluate and manage grazing

Chapter Two examines grazing as a natural process, to which both forage plants and grazing animals are adapted. Grazing is a disturbance, whose effects on plants depend on timing, intensity, and frequency. These are things that can be controlled by management.

Chapter Three addresses the effects of grazing on larger-scale processes, especially the flow of water and nutrients through and across pastures and watersheds. These processes are fundamental to the ecological functioning of rangelands and are equally important to wildlife, livestock, biodiversity, and humans.

Chapter Four examines how the ecological processes described in Chapter Three relate to spatial and temporal scales. Ecological processes are not linear across scales, at least not in Southwestern landscapes where rainfall is limiting and highly

4

unpredictable. Rather, these land-scapes are characterized by critical thresholds of change. Monitoring is necessary to gauge the effects of management decisions efficiently enough that thresholds of degrada-tion are not crossed.

Chapter Five applies these ideas to management. The New Ranch uses planning and monitoring to control the timing, frequency, and intensity of grazing with a view towards preserving and enhancing ecological functioning on the land. It seeks to harness natural processes of recovery and resilience to distur-bance. It embraces both the science and the art of resource management, recognizing the limits of our knowl-edge and seeking always to learn from experience and from the land.

Finally, Chapter Six ad-dresses a not-so-scientific issue: How to "make the leap" to the New Ranch. If ranch-ing is to persist for another century, change cannot be avoided. Better to take the initiative than to have it arrive, uninvited, in the form of debts, lawsuits, regulations, or suburban ranchettes. Effecting change requires careful evaluation of the resources avail-able to manage-ment—money,

people, and the land itself—to identify goals and plan ways of achieving them.

The Conclusion situates New Ranch management in the larger context of issues facing ranchers: the pressures of suburban development and land value escalation; federal environmental regulation; environ-mentalism; and declining rates of return to livestock ranching. Good management is necessary to survive in twenty-first century ranching, but other tools and resources may also be needed.

Finally, numbers in brackets in the text refer to entries in the Bibliography. This seemed the best way to enable readers who seek further information to find it, without cluttering up the text with long lists of names and dates. The Bibliogra-phy may seem long, but it makes no claim to being comprehensive.

Chaining. (Photo courtesy of Sid Goodloe.)

THE CARRIZO VALLEY RANCH
Capitan, New Mexico

"Time-controlled grazing and piñon-juniper control have been the backbone of my management here on Carrizo Valley Ranch..."
--Sid Goodloe

Sid Goodloe's Carrizo Valley Ranch occupies 3,400 acres of private land in a drainage on the east side of the Carrizo Mountains in south-central New Mexico. Elevations range from 6,500 to 7,500 feet, and precipitation averages around nineteen inches, half of which is snowfall. The upper two-thirds of the ranch borders U.S. Forest Service land.

When Sid bought the ranch in the spring of 1956, there was hardly enough feed for the sixty cattle that were grazing there. The vegetation was largely piñon-juniper, blue grama grass, and cholla cactus. At higher elevations, dense stands of young ponderosa pine trees engulfed a handful of much older,

widely spaced junipers. The drainages were dry gullies. That summer the rains never came, so the grama grass didn't grow. Sid spent the following winter burning spines off of the cholla so his cattle could eat the pulp. He cut his herd to forty animals. When ample rains fell the next year, Sid witnessed sheet erosion from the forested areas and powerful floods rushing through the gullies.

Sid researched early accounts of the area and learned that the ranch had once been predominantly grassland at the lower end, and a savanna higher up. Trees had been so exceptional that seldom could one be found for a witness tree at the section corners. Streams running out of the mountains had supplied enough water

Black Grama

for eight homesteads at the turn of the century. Fires had been common. With this vision of the past in his mind, Sid commenced a program of brush removal. He chained 1,700 acres of piñon-juniper, leaving a few trees for shade and larger stands on rockier soils where grasses would be hard to establish. He cut the firewood to sell and burned the slash. Then he seeded the ground with native grasses. With help from the Soil Conservation Service, he built check dams in the eroding gullies to capture water and sediment.

In the higher elevations, Sid is still in the process of thinning the ponderosa pines and using fire to encourage grasses to grow instead of trees. The pines are almost all the same age, having sprouted around 1920 when the Forest Service's fire suppression program became established. Growing in dense stands, they shade the forest floor and prevent grasses from growing, while competition among the trees limits their own growth. Despite their age, few are greater than six inches in diameter. In some areas that Sid thinned in the 1960s, by contrast, trees have grown to more than fifteen inches in diameter in less than forty years. By allowing sunlight to reach the ground, Sid has restored grasses and an understory of oak brush, both of which respond well to fire and provide important feed for cattle, deer, and elk.

In the 1960s, Sid spent two and a half years studying savanna grasslands in Kenya. He returned in

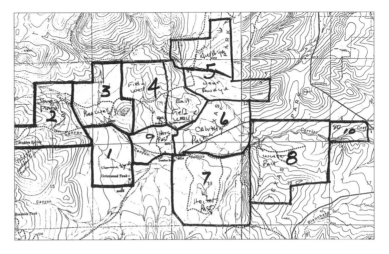

Figure 1. Sid Goodloe's fences divide his ranch into thirteen pastures.

1969 and began applying the lessons he had learned. He implemented a short-duration grazing (SDG) method (see **The Debate Over Short-Duration Grazing**, p. 22), discovered in Rhodesia (now Zimbabwe), where he'd met Allan Savory. Sid published a paper on the method in the November 1969 issue of the *Journal of Range Management [41]*. His ranch was the first SDG operation in the United States.

By the mid-1970s Sid had divided the ranch into thirteen pastures, locating his fences according to topography and water sources (see Figure 1 above).

At present, seven pastures in the higher country are used every summer in a rotation, with each pasture receiving at least six weeks of rest. The rotation begins in a different pasture each year. If the summer rains are good, Sid accelerates the rotation. He has determined that rotation is not necessary in the dormant season, from November to May, when his cattle graze the lower country. He uses three pastures in the

spring and fall, and two in the winter. Each year, one pasture is reserved as a "drought valve," a source of forage in emergency conditions.

Gradually, over ten or twelve years, Sid built his herd up to 100 head. The ranch could support 120 now, he says, but heavier stocking would create more risks during drought periods. His cows are "Alpine Black": three-fourths black angus and one-fourth brown swiss. "Environmentally adapted cattle," he calls them. Their black color absorbs heat from the sun during the winter and protects them from pink eye and blistered udders, which can be a problem when bright sunshine reflects off the snow in the spring. Sid also keeps a couple of longhorn cows in the herd because they are more aggressive in fending off predators.

Sid times the breeding and rotation of his herd to match the rhythms of forage production. High pregnancy rates require that the cows be in peak nutritional condition at the onset of the breeding season. On Sid's ranch, forage conditions peak in early May, when the oak brush begins to leaf out in the higher elevation pastures. He turns his bulls in and begins the rotation at this time. Sid has found that fall fires and early summer browsing encourage the oak brush to produce fresh, green sprouts much favored by cattle and deer alike. Older, undisturbed plants eventually become tough and less palatable. Calving begins in early February,

and Sid feeds a protein supplement from mid-January through the breeding season. By mid-summer the calves are old enough to use the green forage produced by summer rains. Weaning takes place at the beginning of October, just before the first frost reduces the nutritional value of the standing grasses. His cows then have ample time to improve their condition for the winter ahead.

It is probably not possible to determine how much fire, brush removal, and short-duration grazing have each contributed to the changes in the Carrizo Valley watershed. But the changes themselves are dramatic. There was no perennial water in the Carrizo drainage in 1956, and hadn't been for decades. By replacing trees with grasses, Sid has increased water infiltration, raising the water table in the riparian area by three or four feet. Since the mid-1980s the creek has been perennial through most of the ranch, and the water runs clear. The riparian area is grazed briefly in the winter and rests every summer. This allows the vegetation to remain lush without becoming so thick that it might engulf the creek entirely. Wild turkey are abundant in the higher country, as are deer. Elk have increased to the point that Sid is concerned about them overgrazing the land. After more than forty years of work, Sid continues his efforts to restore the Carrizo Valley watershed to something like its pre-1870 conditions.

Chapter One

Ranching as Sustainable Agriculture

"There is probably no more ecologically correct way to raise a pound of red meat protein" than grass-fed beef grazing natural (that is, uncultivated) rangelands. -- *Wes Jackson*

Ranching Can Be Sustainable

To be sustainable, ranching must convert a natural, self-reproducing resource into a profitable commodity without undermining the long-term viability of the resource. In other words, forage that grows naturally must be harvested by livestock in such a way that the forage remains vital year after year. Furthermore, the money received for the livestock must be greater than the money spent to produce them. Because the real price of beef has dropped over the past fifty years, while the cost of inputs has increased, the importance of range conditions for profitability has

grown. During the cattle boom, great profits were made from unsustainable ranching; with the public domain open to all comers, the range resources were basically mined. Today it is increasingly the opposite: ranching must be sustainable if it is to be profitable (see **The Goal: Rangeland Health**, p. 11).

Ranching can be sustainable because rangeland systems can tolerate the disturbance caused by grazing *[18]*. They are *resilient* to grazing, meaning that they can recover from it provided that the disturbance is not too great. For example, grasses and other forage plants are adapted to disturbance,

9

"...disturbance can help some grasses and shrubs to maintain vigor, ..."

whether by grazing animals, insects, or fire. Some portion of their biomass can be removed without damaging their long-term viability. Indeed, disturbance can help some grasses and shrubs to maintain vigor, by removing old leaves that are less efficient at photosynthesis and thereby allowing more sunlight to reach younger, more efficient leaves. We will look further at this in the next chapter.

The impacts of grazing are not limited to the plants that are eaten, however. There are other factors to consider: water, soils, nutrients, other plants, wildlife, and a host of organisms that inter-relate with all of them. Livestock are only one piece of a much larger puzzle that must fit together if ranching is to be sustainable.

Sooner or later, all plant biomass is transformed by some process of consumption or decomposition. It may be eaten by an animal or an insect. It may die, fall over, and decay, or it may burn in a fire. If undisturbed for a long enough time, it may oxidize and eventually turn to dust. In most cases, the plant eventually ends up on the ground in feces or carrion or as litter, where it is consumed by decomposers: fungi, bacteria, invertebrates, and insects that break it down into soil and nutrients available to other, living plants.

Most biomass—as much as ninety percent in some years in desert grasslands—simply dies and is directly consumed by decomposers [121]. That means that only ten percent passes through a primary consumer—cow, deer, elk, bird, whathaveyou—before being decomposed [67]. Decomposers drive the whole system, by processing nutrients for plant growth and by increasing the porosity of soils for aeration and water percolation [120, 122]. And they are abundant: In both Sonoran and Chihuahuan desert grasslands, the mass of termites underground is more than three times the mass of cattle in a typical pasture [121].

Viewed as a whole, sustainable ranching can be understood this way: Livestock convert plant biomass that exceeds the needs of the plants into meat; humans harvest the meat for consumption elsewhere. A small amount of the total energy produced by the range is diverted out of the system. Most of this energy would otherwise be consumed by decomposers. As Wes Jackson has put it: "There is probably no more ecologically correct way to raise a pound of red meat protein" than grass-fed beef grazing natural (that is, uncultivated) rangelands [60].

How can sustainable ranching be accomplished? The growth of forage results from many factors which work together in complex ways. In simple terms, the better they are all working together, the better the system as a whole can recover from disturbances such as grazing. We will examine these inter-relationships in subsequent chapters. For now, suffice it to say that the same ecological processes that sustain productive rangeland for livestock grazing also support wildlife and biological diversity. On Sid Goodloe's ranch, it is not a coincidence that improved conditions for his cattle have attracted wildlife, benefited the riparian area, and reduced erosion. The New Ranch is as much about natural resource management as it is about ranch management.

How can grazing be managed for ecological processes? Here we examine this question and review some of the answers given in the past.

Grazing and the Problem of Scale

The challenge of sustainable ranching may be examined at a number of different scales. At its most basic, it concerns the grazing of individual plants, one by one, by individual animals. We will consider this scale in Chapter Two. On a slightly larger scale, herds of livestock graze pastures or allotments

The Goal: Rangeland Health

What are the goals of the New Ranch? How can we define the desired condition of rangelands? Until very recently, there was no comprehensive answer to these questions. For nearly a century, different agencies employed different standards and measures. Range scientists used their own criteria, while biologists used others.

In 1994, a committee of the National Academy of Sciences published *Rangeland Health: New Methods to Classify, Inventory, and Monitor Rangelands [78]*. They concluded that rangeland health can and should be defined and measured in terms of three criteria:

● **Degree of soil stability and watershed function.** Rangelands should not be eroding, and they should capture and retain water rather than shed it as run-off.

● **Integrity of nutrient cycles and energy flows.** Rangelands should support plants that capture energy from the sun and cycle nutrients from the soil.

● **Presence of functioning recovery mechanisms.** Rangelands should be resistant to extreme disturbances and resilient to change—that is, they should be capable of recovering from more ordinary disturbances.

These may seem rather simple or incomplete, but they are not. They were devised to provide a basis for consistent, national rangeland assessment, relevant and applicable to all present and future publics. This is their value. By understanding rangelands in terms of fundamental ecological processes, these criteria encompass virtually all others we might put forth: wildlife habitat, recreation, food and fiber production, scientific research, education, open space, etc. As a minimum, the potential of the land should be maintained, so that future generations will be able to benefit from it, no matter what that benefit may be.

Much work is being done to refine the criteria of *Rangeland Health* and apply them in the field. But the committee has done a huge service in arriving at a basic framework that all people—ranchers, scientists, environmentalists, recreationalists, agency personnel—can agree on.

"Simply put, a pasture is more than the sum of its individual plants, and a watershed is more than the sum of its individual pastures."

that make up a ranch unit. This is the scale at which most management decisions are taken, and we address it in Chapter Three. On a still larger scale, animals graze within watersheds and landscapes containing many ranches. We will examine this scale in Chapter Four. Each of these scales implies some temporal dimension as well: we can see a change in a grazed plant very quickly; change in a pasture may take a week or more to be evident; changes at the watershed scale may take years to notice.

One might expect that sustainability at the smallest scale would guarantee sustainability at the larger scales. That is, as long as each plant is grazed in a way that does it no long-term damage, then the pasture as a whole will be sustainable; if every ranch is sustainable, then the watershed will be, too. This is true in theory, but problematic in practice, for two reasons:

(1) No one has yet devised a way to control how each animal grazes each plant on the range. Management decisions must be taken on larger scales.

(2) Larger scales are not simply the sum of many smaller ones.

The second point is critically important, and it requires some elaboration. Simply put, a pasture is more than the sum of its individual plants, and a watershed is more than the sum of its individual pastures. This is because the ecological processes that sustain the whole system operate on multiple scales

simultaneously [26]. When one plant is grazed, neighboring plants may gain a competitive advantage because the pool of resources (water, sunlight, nutrients) is larger in scale than individual plants. Vegetation changes elsewhere in the watershed may alter patterns of run-off and erosion, leading to changes downstream, because the water cycle unfolds on a watershed scale. After a large fire in 1995 removed the vegetation from the Forest Service lands above Sid Goodloe's ranch , a torrential storm filled his tanks with sediment, even though his own land did not burn or erode. We will encounter other examples of this later on.

Similar problems arise in going from a shorter to a longer scale of time. The same grazing pressure may produce different results in a year of good rainfall than in a drought year. Last year's rainfall, or a drought five years ago, may affect this year's forage crop. Sid Goodloe's work is a response to overgrazing and other activities that occurred more than half a century ago.

This problem—how to move from one scale to another in the management of grazing—has eluded our understanding for a long time. Scientists have only recently begun to propose solutions to it [20].

Conventional Range Management Tools and Their Limitations

A great deal of work in range science has gone into designing tools that assess conditions at a particular

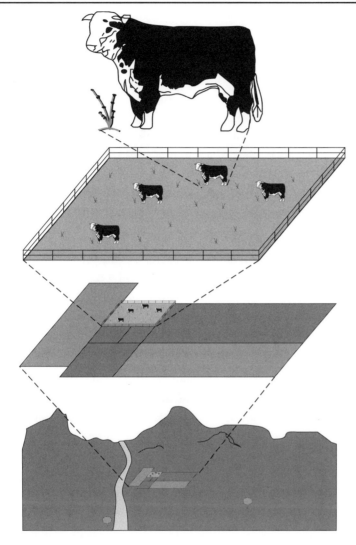

a. **Individual Plant Scale**. An animal grazes the plant at a particular moment in time. Impact is conspicuous, but diminishes as the plant recovers over a period of several weeks (during the growing season) or months.

b. **Pasture Scale** (many plants). Herd of animals grazes over a period of several days to a season, or longer. Impacts develop gradually.

c. **Ranch Scale** (many pastures). Herd or herds of animals graze on an ongoing basis. Impacts unfold over a period of years.

d. **Watershed or Landscape Scale** (many ranches). Multiple herds of animals, grazing ongoing, but impacts and conditions vary from ranch to ranch and year to year. Overall impacts may be difficult to evaluate, given the variety of conditions; change may be noticeable only over a period of many years or decades.

Scale involves two elements: *grain* and *extent*. Grain is the smallest unit of analysis, and extent is the total area from which data are gathered. If your grain is small (individual plants, for example), it's very difficult to have a large extent (a watershed), because you'd have to look at every single plant over a huge area. Thus, as extent expands, grain typically expands as well.

Each scale lends itself to examining certain questions about the impacts of grazing. At scale (a), for example, one can study the effects of grazing on a given plant or compare those effects from one plant to another. At scale (b), one might examine the composition or net production of a community of plants, and so on.

There is also a typical temporal extent for each scale. At scale (a), one can examine change over a period of days or weeks, or at most the lifespan of the plant. Change at the larger scales can only be observed over longer time periods.

Most range science has been done at scales (b) and (c), looking at the effects of grazing on pastures and ranches over periods of one grazing season to several years. Scales (a) and (d) have been studied mostly by other branches of biology and ecology.

Difficulties arise in trying to move from one scale to another, because the relations between scales are not necessarily linear, over space or time. The processes that influence plant growth occur at many scales simultaneously. Broadly speaking, we will look at scale (a) in Chapter Two, scales (b) and (c) in Chapter Three, and scale (d) in Chapter Four. It is important to remember, however, that these scales interact in complex ways that are not fully understood by science.

Figure 2. The Various Scales at which Grazing may be Analyzed and Understood.

"...range utilization makes the same error as carrying capacity: it assumes that something measured at one scale can then be applied to another scale by simple mathematical equations."

scale and then extrapolate the results to other scales. Take carrying capacity, for example. Carrying capacity is typically used at the pasture or ranch scale, with animal units calculated in months or years. Early researchers defined it as the amount of grazing an area could support in the worst (that is, driest) years, so that better years would always allow the range to improve *[43]*. Today, the official carrying capacity of a given area is usually less than what could be supported in good years, but more than what is sustainable in severe drought years.

Carrying capacity is generally calculated by assessing a small area, then multiplying the result by the total area in question. Every rancher and researcher knows that the area you choose to assess makes a big difference to the final result. Aside from this difficulty is another: the result is almost always expanded across time, as a guideline for stocking rates for years to come. Carrying capacity implies some fixed level of productivity, when in fact productivity varies widely from year to year.

This is not to say that carrying capacity is meaningless or unimportant. If a rancher is unwilling to adjust stocking rates frequently, range research suggests stocking the ranch at 90 percent of its official capacity: this yields higher profits and runs fewer risks than stocking at 100 percent *[123]*. But it is important to recognize the limits of carrying capacity as a management tool. It cannot help in managing ecological processes that operate on smaller or larger spatial scales (individual plants, areas within pastures, or entire watersheds) or shorter or longer temporal scales (timing of rainfall within the growing season, for example, or the effects of long-term drought).

An alternative to carrying capacity is range utilization: measuring the percentage of new biomass harvested. Utilization is implicit in carrying capacity, since carrying capacity calculations originally assumed that a fixed proportion of forage plants (usually fifty or fifty-five percent) could sustainably be harvested by livestock. But utilization appears to be a more precise tool, since it works on smaller spatial and temporal scales. It has the advantage of recognizing that forage production varies from year to year, and in theory it looks more closely at individual plants. Recent research suggests that on arid and semiarid rangelands, utilization rates of 30 to 35 percent result in range improvement, while utilization of around 40 percent results in little or no change to key forage plants *[56]*. These figures are significantly less than assumed in early carrying capacity estimates.

Range utilization also has limitations as a management tool, however. Range scientists have disputed how, or even if, it can be quantitatively measured *[14]*. Grazing animals do not graze all plant species evenly, so choosing which plants to measure is an important issue. Pastures are rarely uniform in the rate of growth of plants or the impact of grazing on plants. And grazing itself affects growth rates, meaning that an ungrazed area may be an inaccurate baseline for estimating harvest. Finally, there is the question of when one should measure utilization: at the end of the grazing period, or at the end of the growing season, when grazed plants may have re-grown significantly (see **Misunderstandings about Utilization Rates,** p. 29.) These problems have led some range scientists to argue that range utilization is an inoperable, misleading, or even meaningless tool for management *[94]*.

If it were feasible to control the grazing of individual plants, then managing for some target utilization rate might make sense. But absent that degree of control, range utilization makes the same error as carrying capacity: it assumes that something measured at one scale can then be applied to another scale by simple mathematical equations.

A third tool commonly used to evaluate range management is range condition. This tool compares present vegetation at a site with the site's "potential" vegetation and assigns a score based on how similar they are. The "potential" vegetation

Contrast between Sid Goodloe's ranch on the right and Forest Service land on the left, which shows the encroachment of piñon-juniper on the untreated public land. (Photo courtesy of Sid Goodloe.)

is generally assumed to be that which existed prior to western ranching, the so-called climax community (or subclimax maintained by fire). When it was developed, range condition further assumed that reductions in grazing pressure would cause succession, meaning a shift back towards the site's potential vegetation community *[85]*. As noted already, this last assumption has proved to be false in many arid or semiarid rangelands *[36, 101]*. There appear to be many other variables besides grazing pressure that affect vegetation over space and time. Even in areas where the successional model holds true, there remains a need to refine what is meant by grazing pressure, which is typically understood in terms of the tools already discussed: carrying capacity or range utilization.

Disturbance

The shortcomings of these range management tools are especially pronounced in arid and semiarid settings, where rainfall is both scarce and highly irregular *[14]*. The productivity of these rangelands varies widely across space and time. Which plants grow, and how much they

The results on Sid Goodloe's land from a stand replacement fire on public land above. That fire was caused by fuel build-up from years of fire suppression. (Photo courtesy of Sid Goodloe.)

grow, depends not only on how much rain falls but when and how quickly it falls, and on the weather that follows it. Rainfall is notoriously spotty, especially during the summer. Droughts are a normal part of the climate. Until the twentieth century, fires were also normal *[76]*.

These are "disturbance-prone" ecosystems, adapted to withstand droughts, fires, floods, and other extreme stresses *[26]* (see **More on Disturbance**, p. 17). Symptoms of this include high biodiversity and a high degree of variation over space and time. Because water and nutrients are scarce, plants survive much closer to their limits of tolerance than in other areas. Often they survive by exploiting unique features of a particular location, where other plants cannot compete as well. So for example, even on a small hill, you'll find different plants on the north-facing side than on the south-facing side, and different plants on top than at the bottom. Small differences in temperature, soil, or moisture availability produce large differences in vegetation. The result is a landscape of many different plants, each suited to particular conditions of slope, aspect, soil, temperature, and so on.

Unpredictable climate patterns reinforce this opportunistic tendency. Plants must be able to withstand disturbances like drought and take advantage of rain when it finally arrives. Different plants will grow depending on whether the rain arrives in summer or winter, in large quantities or small. Over thousands of years of evolution, the vegetation of these areas has adapted to reflect these circumstances. The common tools of range management were not designed to handle so much variability *[101]*.

So how is sustainable ranching to be achieved, particularly in arid and semiarid systems? New tools are needed, tools that do not

16

More on Disturbance

Grazing is a disturbance—what does this mean? A number of definitions of "disturbance" have been proposed by ecologists, and the precise meaning has not been completely resolved *[54]*. Put in simple terms, disturbances are events that disrupt ecosystems. Depending on the definition and the scale of analysis, a disturbance could be as isolated as a lightning strike that removes a large tree and opens up a space where other plants find a niche to grow. A flood that scours the vegetation from a streambed would be a slightly larger disturbance. Disturbances that can vary in extent would include wildfires, very strong winds that blow over stands of trees, unusually severe extremes of temperature, or an outbreak of disease or insects. Finally, at the largest scales, severe drought or even global climate change could be considered disturbances.

Part of the difficulty in defining disturbance is that it always implies some notion of "normal" conditions. All natural systems experience change, and change almost always occurs, at least in part, in response to some kind of random or unusual event. So one might argue that disturbance is itself normal. If lightning strikes occur with clock-like regularity in a given forest, should they count as a disturbance? What about prolonged "events," like drought? Here again, the spatial and temporal scale of analysis is critical *[40]*. It may turn out that the definition of disturbance will vary, depending on the ecosystem in question. Fortunately, we do not need to resolve this issue here, because grazing is unquestionably a disturbance according to all the proposed definitions.

All disturbances affect vegetation, either directly or indirectly. Furthermore, the severity of all disturbances can be understood in terms of timing, intensity, and frequency (for some, like wildfires or volcanic eruptions, size is another important variable) *[26]*. Ecologists hypothesize that intermediate levels of disturbance (in frequency and intensity) result in the greatest diversity of species in any given system *[24, 54]*. That is, disturbances can increase or decrease diversity, just as they can benefit or harm any given plant species *[108]*. Where two disturbances interact, results can be surprising. In a study in Oklahoma, research found that diversity was highest in areas that were both burned and grazed, and lowest in areas that burned but weren't grazed. Unburned, ungrazed areas had an intermediate level of diversity *[24]*.

Southwestern desert grasslands are unusually prone to disturbance, for a number of reasons. The scarcity of water and nutrients imposes austere conditions on most plant species, so that even rather minor disturbances may have significant effects. Dry, hot conditions and intense lightning make fires common at certain times of year. Combine these factors with diverse topography and extreme variability in rainfall, both spatially and temporally, and you get ecosystems that have selected for plants capable of surviving frequent and/ or severe disturbance, either individually or by reproducing very opportunistically. These are also the conditions that make some changes difficult or impossible to reverse in practical terms: If a disturbance is severe enough, it may alter soils or hydrology in ways that nature cannot recover in anything like a human timeframe.

(con't on p. 18)

More on Disturbance *(con't from p. 17)*

For land management purposes, disturbances are important because: (1) they can occur randomly or unpredictably, as with a wildfire or drought; and (2) their effects can vary widely, especially when two or more disturbances overlap or coincide. For example, wildfires have different effects depending on when they occur (early or late in the growing season) *[75]*. The effects of grazing may resemble those of fire, or be quite different, depending on circumstances *[10]*. And grazing during a drought period is a much more intense disturbance than during a wet period. Southwestern rangelands were severely damaged in the 1890s and early 1900s when two disturbances coincided: drought and very heavy grazing. Either one without the other would not have been nearly as damaging. These considerations make effective planning and flexible management both very difficult and very important.

To say that grazing is a disturbance is thus to focus attention on ecological processes, some of which exceed our understanding (let alone our control). Compared to many disturbances, livestock grazing is easy to control, in all of its dimensions (timing, intensity, and frequency). Its current effects on vegetation, moreover, are much smaller than its historic effects, because numbers are smaller and management is better than they were, say, one hundred years ago *[76]*. In short, grazing can be good, bad, or indifferent for ecosystems, depending on the details.

assume that larger scales are simple multiples of smaller ones.

The ranches profiled here suggest a new way of thinking about grazing, one that looks at the ecological processes that sustain plant growth. Measuring the composition or productivity of grasses in a pasture can tell us a lot, especially over many years. But it cannot give us an understanding of the long-term viability of the forage, because it does not look at what makes the plants grow—namely, the cycles of nutrients, water, and energy. These processes work across scales of space and time. By looking at the processes themselves, we do not commit ourselves to any assump-

tions about scale. The purpose of the following chapters is to explain how ecological processes relate to grazing at various scales and how grazing can be managed for them.

We will see that the ranchers like Sid Goodloe who have succeeded in improving the condition of their lands—for cattle and also for wildlife, riparian areas, and water—use tools that match the way the land itself works. *The effects of disturbances on the land depend on timing (when they happen), intensity (how severe they are), and frequency (how often they recur). Grazing is a disturbance which can be managed in these terms.*

THE OGILVIE CATTLE COMPANY AND THE U BAR RANCH

Silver City and Gila, New Mexico

"The [Southwestern Willow Flycatcher] study on U Bar Ranch demonstrates that livestock grazing can be compatible and even complementary to sustaining some habitats."

--David Ogilvie

David Ogilvie is owner-manager of the Ogilvie Cattle Company and manager of the U Bar Ranch. The family ranch is about 15,000 acres, 70 percent of it private land. The U Bar Ranch is much larger: roughly 290 sections, including 70 sections of deeded land and almost 100 sections of Forest Service leases. Elevations range from 4,900 to 7,500 feet; average annual precipitation is about 16 inches.

David practices rest/rotation grazing. He has divided the family ranch into eighteen pastures. He keeps his cattle in a herd, rotating them through sixteen pastures during the growing season. The other two pastures—which amount to almost half the ranch—are grazed only in the winter, dormant season. Rotation is also an important part of management of the U Bar.

David's goal is to allow all of his pastures to go to seed every year. Grazing periods during the growing season range from one to four weeks, after which a pasture rests for roughly a year. The last pasture used during the growing season may not recover until the following year, but then again, it may have already set seed before the grazing period began. The following year's rotation will be different, to ensure that the pasture will not receive the same impact every year. David believes that recovery is a more important management goal than any target of utilization. Sometimes he will use as much as 70 percent of the standing forage in a pasture, as long as the rest period that follows is long enough to ensure that the grasses recover (see **Misunderstandings About Utilization Rates**, p. 29).

The fenceline photo on p. 24

Kentucky Bluegrass

19

David Ogilvie, Scott Stoleson of the Rocky Mountain Research Station, and others on U Bar Ranch's Southwestern Willow Flycatcher habitat. (Photo courtesy of Courtney White.)

illustrates the dramatic effects of growing season recovery. On the left side the grass is tall and thick; on the right side it looks heavily grazed. If you looked at the two sides only in terms of stocking rate, you'd think that the right side was much more heavily grazed than the left. But the opposite is the case. The stocking rate for the left pasture was fifteen times greater than on the right; adjusted for the length of the grazing period, grazing pressure was almost four times greater. The dramatic difference between the two sides of the fence is a function of timing: The left pasture was grazed at the beginning of the growing season, in May 1999. The right pasture was grazed at the end of the growing season, in August 1999. The photo was taken in January 2000.

Like Sid Goodloe, David is concerned about the spread of piñon-juniper and the consequent decline in grasses on his ranch. He has witnessed this invasion over the past thirty years, especially in higher areas and up into the nearby Forest Service lands. He attributes an increase in flooding and sedimentation in lower areas (including both his family ranch and the U Bar) to the replacement of grasses by trees higher in the watersheds. To address this problem, he has implemented a burn program on his ranch. Fires in July 1997 and April 1999 burned about one section of land. He rested the areas for three growing seasons prior to burning,

to allow a fuel load to accumulate. Even so, the fires were very patchy. In some areas piñon-juniper mortality was very high, in others not. Where large bear grass plants grew at the base of junipers, mortality was almost 100 percent, because the bear grass burned very hot. The immediate response to burning was a flush of annual grasses and forbs, as well as fresh sprouts on browse species like willow, sumac, and mulberry. Perennial grasses have gradually colonized areas of bare ground where pinon-juniper stood before. David has observed an increase in elk and deer on the burned areas.

Endangered species are a major issue on the U Bar. The ranch manages private lands along a nine-mile reach of the Gila River, most of which is grazed and/or farmed. The land is nesting habitat for the largest known population of Southwestern Willow Flycatchers, and large numbers of Spike Dace and Loach Minnow have recently been found in the river. All three are federally listed endangered species. On the Gila National Forest, upstream and downstream of the U Bar land, cattle have been excluded from the riparian area in behalf of these species. Yet populations have not been found to date on the Forest. The grazed and farmed lands, on the other hand, have seen a significant increase in Willow Flycatchers since surveys began in 1994. The U Bar has partnered with scientists from the Rocky Mountain Research Station and Western New Mexico University to conduct detailed research on the endangered species, and it appears that the Willow Flycatcher may prefer habitats that have been modified by grazing and farming activities. David manages these lands with the bird's needs in mind, grazing mostly in the dormant season and minimizing farm work during the nesting season.

Chapter Two

Grazing as a Natural Process

"Ranching is one of the few Western occupations that have been renewable and have produced a continuing way of life."
--Wallace Stegner

Grasses and Grazers: An Evolutionary Perspective

Range management defines grazing as the consumption of standing forage (grasses and edible forbs) by livestock or wildlife *[56]*. More generally, grazing can be equated with herbivory, or the process by which animals consume plants to acquire energy and nutrients *[110]*. In this chapter, we consider the direct effects of grazing on plants. In the next chapter, we will examine the indirect effects.

Grazing is a natural process which has been occurring for millions of years. From the fossil record, it has been determined that grasses and grazers evolved together some 45 million years ago, and that both spread significantly during the Miocene period *[81]*.

Having coevolved, grazers and grasses are adapted to each other. Grazing animals have developed the physiological capacity to derive energy from plant material that humans and most other mammals cannot directly consume. Grasses have developed the capacity to recover from grazing (and other disturbances common to their environments, like fire). Some scientists argue that grasses and grazers exist in a mutualistic relationship: From the perspective of evolution, one would not be possible without the other *[81]*.

Examples of this mutualism

The Debate Over Short-Duration Grazing

Three of the six ranches profiled in this manual practice short-duration grazing (SDG), year-round or at least during the growing season; the other three utilize rotational systems with longer, flexible grazing periods. Given the large amount of scientific research that has been done on SDG in recent decades, and the controversies that still surround it, the subject warrants a brief discussion.

The two most tested claims of SDG concern water infiltration and stocking rates. Multiple studies have found that SDG does not increase infiltration rates (as proponents claim) or reduce sedimentation compared to continuous grazing at moderate stocking rates *[29, 38, 87, 103, 104, 112, 113, 114, 115]*. Studies have also disputed the claim that SDG makes possible sudden, dramatic increases in stocking rates *[97, 105]*. Research into other factors, such as forage production or animal gain, have found inconsistent results or no difference between continuous and rotational systems at the same stocking rates *[2, 22, 39, 45, 48, 63, 80, 84, 109, 111]*.

Taking these results as conclusive, some prominent scientists have published unequivocal judgments against SDG and in favor of continuous grazing at moderate stocking rates *[57, 58, 59, 86]*. They argue that "the selection of the correct stocking rate is the most important range management decision." This appears to be true, but numerous questions remain. Given that forage production varies widely over time, the "correct stocking rate" probably changes too. How often should a rancher revisit this question? Moreover, how are we to explain the experiences of ranchers like Goodloe, Bowe, and Winder (see **The Carrizo Valley Ranch**, p. 6, **The Rafter F Cattle Company**, p. 45, and **The Beck Land and Cattle Company**, p. 59)? Where should we draw the line between SDG and flexible rotational strategies? What about the many other aspects of SDG that remain neither proved nor disproved by controlled experiments?

This handbook seeks to stand apart from the SDG debate, for two reasons. First, the evidence is quite plainly inconclusive. Both sides have facts: The scientists have results from controlled, replicated experiments; successful SDG ranchers have land, photos, monitoring data, and persuasive stories. (Although there are also stories of ranchers who have tried SDG without success.)

Presumably, the facts only conflict because we don't yet know how to explain them fully. Perhaps the theory behind SDG is poorly suited to experimental methods. The scientists have typically imposed fixed conditions in their experiments—unchanging stocking rates and rotation schedules, for example—while the SDG ranchers insist that flexibility is critical, since conditions change from season to season and year to year. (Many stress that SDG is not a "system" at all, but rather a way of making decisions *[92, 93]*.) Furthermore, experiments tend to isolate discrete components of range ecosystems to test (water infiltration rates, vegetation cover or composition, or livestock production, for example). The SDG ranchers believe that the whole cannot be so easily reduced to particular parts. Finally, much of the research has tested SDG using very high stocking rates, potentially confounding the effects of intensity and timing.

(con't on p. 23)

The Debate Over Short-Duration Grazing *(con't from p. 22)*

Second, the debate itself does little to improve management on the ground. Scholarly disagreement is good for science, but it can lead to confusion and gridlock among ranchers and agency personnel. Understandably, bureaucrats feel a need to have "the science" on their side, especially if they may end up in court defending their decisions. The literature on stocking rates is less equivocal, so they feel compelled to rely on stocking rates as their principal management tool. This effectively removes other tools (such as changing the timing or frequency of grazing) that could help resolve differences. When the only available tool is cutting stocking rates, resistance from the lessee is virtually guaranteed.

Given the tremendous variability of rangelands, especially in the Southwest, it is unlikely that any one system will ever be found to be the "right" one everywhere. The goal here is not to resolve the debate over SDG, but to articulate some principles that are consistent both with the preponderance of our present scientific knowledge and with the experiences of successful ranchers *[46]*. One such principle is that the effects of grazing cannot be reduced to a single variable. Timing, intensity, and frequency are all important. Viewed this way, SDG and rotational grazing have a lot in common: Both seek to control the timing and frequency (as well as the intensity) of grazing to ensure that plants recover. Another principle is that management must constantly adapt to changing conditions. Adding or removing stock is an important dimension of adaptability—perhaps the most important—but it is not the only one.

The overarching need is for continued learning and studying and experimenting, not just by academic researchers but by ranch managers, who know their land well and who have the strongest incentive to improve it. Critics of SDG sometimes argue that its successes are not due to the grazing system itself, but to the more conscientious and observant management that sometimes accompanies it *[86]*. This may well be right. But if so, we must then ask what kind of management SDG inspires.

are plentiful in research conducted on wild grazers in their native habitats. Studies of the Serengeti Plain in eastern Africa, for example, have found that grazing increases forage quality and its rate of production. Plots excluded from grazing undergo rapid shifts in vegetation growth and composition, usually becoming less diverse *[73]*. It appears that the plants and animals of the Serengeti benefit from each other even as they compete for resources *[71]*. Other research has examined mutualism between lesser snow geese and the vegetation of salt marshes in Manitoba *[52]*. The great bison herds of North America appear to have had a mutualistic relationship with the prairies found there *[53]*.

What exactly makes these relationships mutually beneficial? Scientists have yet to answer this question conclusively. Many experiments have been done to simulate grazing by clipping tissue from plants

Fenceline contrast on the Ogilvie Ranch. The pasture on the left is 100 acres in size and carried 275 head of livestock for one week. The pasture on the right is 1,500 acres; it supported the same herd for four weeks. Grazing pressure was therefore much greater in the left pasture. The difference is timing: the left pasture has had a growing season to recover, while the right pasture has not. (Photo by the author.)

with scissors and carefully studying how they respond. Results are mixed. Some grasses appear to compensate for the tissue loss by growing more quickly afterwards. But a great deal depends on how much tissue is lost, when it is lost in the plant's life cycle, and whether clipping occurs only once or multiple times. There are also questions about whether these experiments accurately simulate real world conditions.

The scientific dispute over mutualism and "compensatory photosynthesis" is in one sense a result of the problem of scale described in the previous chapter. If we look at the smallest scale, where an individual plant is grazed by an animal, then grazing appears to be a damaging disturbance: the plant loses tissue and gets little or nothing in return. Whether or not it compen-

sates for the loss, the plant would probably have been better off avoiding it in the first place. There are, of course, many plants that have evolved a means of doing just that: spines or chemical compounds that deter grazing animals from biting them. Critics of the mutualism thesis agree that grasses can *tolerate* grazing (just as they can tolerate other disturbances), but they reject the notion that plants have adapted to *benefit* from being grazed *[9, 11]*.

Scientists who support the mutualism thesis tend to look at larger scales *[72, 74]*. Individual plants may lose tissue but simultaneously benefit from the larger effects of grazing on, for example, nutrient availability *[53]*. These benefits may operate over longer time scales, affecting the persistence of communities of plants rather than individuals. Grazing occurs in a larger context and cannot be understood simply as a relationship between one plant and one animal. We will return to this issue in the next chapter.

Wild vs. Domestic Grazing

There is a more practical issue to deal with here. How do wild grazers graze, and do domesticated livestock graze in the same ways? Most range forage species are adapted to tolerate a certain kind of grazing, typical of large herds of wild ungulates. Such grazing is characterized by an acute period of impact followed by a longer period of rest. For example, herds of bison on the Great Plains moved into an area of good forage, impacted it severely, then moved on to another area. They did not return until good forage was again present. Similarly with snow geese, which graze the salt marshes of Manitoba only in the summer before migrating south for the winter *[52]*. Most large wild animals move when local food supplies give out; if they cannot find food, they die, thereby giving the plants a chance to recover.

Domestic livestock cannot usually move so easily, at least not without management intervention. Jim Winder (see **The Beck Land and Cattle Company**, p. 59) compares destocking to migration: It removes grazing pressure when local forage conditions are inadequate to support his cattle. Keeping livestock confined on forage they would otherwise abandon creates the conditions for a kind of grazing that departs from the natural patterns to which grasses are adapted.

No one has yet been able to define precisely where the difference between "natural" and "unnatural" grazing lies. One study compared the grazing pressure of wild herbivores in the Serengeti with that of domestic livestock in South America. Measured regionally, the wild animals place only one-tenth as much demand on the forage base as do domestic livestock (in terms of total biomass of herbivores per unit of primary productivity of forage) *[79]*. A wild herd may be huge, and it may be concentrated in a small area at any given moment. But relative to its overall range—most of which is ungrazed most of the time—the herd's pressure on the land is less than that of domestic animals, spread more evenly over an equivalent area. Nevertheless, evidence of compensatory growth has been found with domestic livestock grazing *[77]*. The densities of livestock, then, might be considered "unnaturally" high for arid and semiarid rangelands, but this does not mean that grazing *per se* is unnatural. It simply magnifies the importance of understanding the multitude of other factors that affect the interaction between grazers and plants.

The Grazing Animal

Consider the matter first from the point of view of the grazing animal. It is well known that grazers do not graze every plant. Wild and domesticated animals both graze selectively. They will graze some species in preference to others, as every rancher knows. Grazers will also select among plants of the same species, choosing to graze some and not others. What they graze depends, further, on what else is available at a given time and place. Many ranchers in southern Arizona have found that

"No one has yet been able to define precisely where the difference between 'natural' and 'unnatural' grazing lies."

Slopes at the beginning of reclamation of an overburden pile at a mine site near Cuba, New Mexico. (Photo courtesy of Courtney White.)

and herds adjust to local conditions—those that don't are usually culled. Calves generally follow their mothers' example in what and when to graze.

Cattle turned into a pasture for the first time will graze differently—and usually with less success—than cattle that have become accustomed to the pasture and its vegetation. Low calving rates are common among replacement heifers in the first year, if they have been brought in from other ranges. In the second year, calving rates rise. Ranchers who change management systems have to educate their cattle, so to speak, to work within the new patterns of water and forage availability.

Finally, grazing animals compete for forage with other grazing species (cattle and elk, for example) and with each other. Older cows may effectively prevent younger cows from having access to the most desirable forage. Cattle grouped together in a herd interact differently with each other, with predators, and with the plants they graze compared to cattle spread out thinly over a pasture.

All of these variables make it difficult to generalize about the way animals graze plants. There are simply too many variables, and science has not yet discovered how to control for them all in measuring the impacts of grazing. Managing

their cattle will graze Lehmann lovegrass at the beginning and the end of the growing season, because little else is green at that time. But when the native grasses are green, cattle tend to ignore the Lehmann.

What gets grazed depends, also, on what the grazing animal needs at the time. A lactating cow has different nutritional needs from a dry cow, and will graze differently as a result. Sid Goodloe's decision to manage for fresh oak sprouts in May reflects the seasonal nature of plant and animal growth alike.

Grazing is both an instinctive behavior and a learned process. All ranchers know that different breeds and ages of cattle have different grazing habits. Some are better adapted to hot, dry environments than others; some are more likely to climb hillsides or to travel away from water to graze. But breeding and age do not control these behaviors entirely. Individuals

grazing remains as much an art as a science.

The Grazed Plant

Things are somewhat more clearly defined when viewed from the perspective of the plants (although scientists have many questions here, as well). For plants, grazing is a disturbance, an external pressure with acute effects. The effects vary depending on the plant species, but for grasses in general three factors are paramount: when the plant is grazed, how much of it is grazed, and how soon it is grazed again.

Imagine a perennial grass plant over the course of a year. Whenever water or heat are insufficient, the plant is dormant. It is alive, but photosynthesis is not occurring. Below ground, its roots may be forming buds, but above ground the leaves are brown. The plant is not producing food for itself. It is not growing. Grazing during the dormant season is unlikely to cause damage, because the leaves are not living tissue at this time.

When moisture and temperature conditions reach certain levels (different for different species of grass), the plant enters a period of growth. Photosynthesis may occur for only a few minutes a day, or for many hours during the main growing season. Below ground, the plant's roots begin to grow, drawing

Cows reclaiming an overburden pile at a mine site near Cuba, New Mexico. (Photo courtesy of Courtney White.)

minerals and nutrients from the soil. Above ground, the leaves begin to "green up," beginning at the base of the plant. New leaves form and some portion of the old leaves regenerate, turning from brown to green.

In commencing to grow, the plant utilizes stored energy to produce new above-ground growth. It thus takes a risk, so to speak, that the new leaves will be able to produce enough additional energy to replenish its supplies. At this early stage of growth, then, the plant is more vulnerable to leaf loss than it is later in the growing season.

Throughout the growing season, the plant responds to changing conditions of moisture and sunlight. If conditions permit, the plant continues photosynthesis through the growing season until temperatures drop again in the fall. (This is a big "if," one we will examine more closely in the next

Revegetated slope at Cuba mine site, after first year of reclamation: an example of the use of animal impact for restoration. (Photo courtesy of Courtney White.)

mouths, and they will not defoliate a plant completely unless there is no other feed available. The majority of plant biomass in grasslands is actually below ground, completely beyond the reach of grazers.

Grasses have several traits that enable them to tolerate grazing, and in some circumstances to benefit from it [19]. Most importantly, they produce more leaf area than is necessary for optimal photosynthesis, meaning that some leaf area can be removed without damage to their growth and reproduction. Younger leaves photosynthesize more efficiently than older ones, and defoliation of older leaves can expose younger leaves to greater sunlight. Many grasses have growth points very close to ground level, where they are unlikely to be bitten off by large-mouthed grazers like cattle. Grasses are adapted to fire in a similar way: all the plant parts needed for resprouting and surviving a fire are at or below ground level, protected from flames and heat.

These traits do not control the effects of grazing on a plant, however [17]. Grazing disturbs the plant by removing leaf tissue. This can be good, bad, or indifferent for the plant as a whole, depending on when the disturbance occurs (timing), how severe it is (intensity), and whether the plant is disturbed again (frequency). If very little leaf is removed, the effects of grazing may be negligible. A more severe, single grazing may slow growth in the

chapter.) It produces enough food to support growth in the roots and the leaves, as well as to develop tillers and/or seed stalks. It stores up energy for the upcoming dormant season. It flowers and sets seed. Eventually the plant returns to dormancy, its leaves again turning brown. The health or vigor of the plant depends on its ability to produce enough food during the growing season to survive through the dormant season and resume growth when conditions are again favorable.

Grazing is a Disturbance that Grasses Tolerate

Grazing removes biomass from individual plants, one plant at a time. In extreme conditions, a grazing animal may remove nearly all of the plant's above-ground growth, but normally this does not occur. Cattle can barely graze closer than an inch or two to the ground because of the shape of their

Misunderstandings About Utilization Rates

Utilization rates seem straightforward enough: They measure the percentage of above-ground biomass harvested by livestock. The old rule of thumb was "take half, leave half," which would mean a utilization rate of fifty percent—right?

Not necessarily. Properly understood, utilization rates measure the percentage of use of *annual* herbage production. If a pasture is grazed year-around, then "take half, leave half" is fifty percent utilization. But if grazing occurs only in the dormant season, or stops before the end of the growing season, "take half, leave half" is less than fifty percent. Why? Because the grasses grow back when given growing-season rest. Indeed, they may grow back almost completely, such that "take half, leave half" could mean almost zero percent utilization. In short, utilization rates can only be measured at the *end* of the growing season.

The limitations of utilization rates for grazing management are discussed in Chapter Five. Here, a couple of practical problems should be mentioned. First, managing for a particular utilization rate is always attended by a measure of uncertainty, because no one can know precisely how much longer the grasses will have sufficient energy and moisture to grow. An early frost or a dry late summer might result in an unexpectedly high rate of utilization by curtailing recovery, even in the absence of further grazing. This kind of uncertainty can easily cause problems between a rancher and agency officials. They may agree to a target utilization rate, but then find themselves at odds at mid-summer, if it looks like the target has been reached. Will continued growth balance out further grazing, or not? It's hard to say until later, by which time it may be too late.

Second, wildlife managers have embraced utilization rates for another reason: to ensure that sufficient cover is maintained for quail or other species that live, feed, or breed on the ground. Wildlife managers may not understand the temporal dimension of utilization rates, or at least they may define utilization differently than range scientists do. The miscommunication that ensues may lead to frustration and distrust. So if you do decide to manage for some rate of utilization, be sure that you and everyone else are clear about how and when it will be measured.

roots, and/or accelerate the growth of leaves, but recovery is likely if grazing does not recur for one to two growing seasons. Repeated defoliations in the same growing season, however, can set the plant back for many years to come *[107]*. These effects also depend on the plant species in question.

Until recently, it was believed that grazing caused grasses to direct energy stored in their roots up into leaf growth, just as occurs at the beginning of the growing season. More recent research suggests that this is not the case, although the precise mechanisms of recovery remain obscure. For now, the best conclusion available is that *the more leaf area that remains after grazing,*

Roger Bowe's herd concentrated on the Rafter F Ranch. (Photo courtesy of Roger Bowe.)

the growing season requires close monitoring of key forage species. Once a plant has set seed, its growth for the season is largely complete.

● **Intensity**. The more leaf area that is removed, the more slowly the plant will be able to recover. How much leaf area is removed depends on grazing pressure: how many animals are present, of what kind, and for how long.

● **Frequency**. A plant that is grazed multiple times during a single season must recommence recovery each time, and will suffer compared to plants grazed only once or twice. Full recovery includes both above- and below-ground growth. Plants that are grazed too frequently will eventually have less root mass, and produce correspondingly less leaf tissue. This leaves them more susceptible to damage from drought or other subsequent disturbance.

Whether plants recover from grazing also depends on larger climatic conditions, of course. During severe drought, water may become so limiting that plants are unable to grow, meaning that recovery from grazing is effectively impossible. Long-term research conducted on the Jornada Experimental Range near Las Cruces, New Mexico, found that the severe drought of the 1950s largely eliminated black grama grass, even in areas where no grazing occurred. (In

faster recovery occurs [16]. Obviously, recovery can only occur when the plant is growing; for most perennial forage species, active growth occurs for only a small portion of the year.

Timing, Intensity, Frequency

From this simple account of the growth of a single grass plant, it is clear that the effects of grazing vary tremendously. The principal factors are:

● **Timing**. Grazing during the dormant season is unlikely to affect the plant's prospects the following spring, because the animal is removing non-photosynthetic tissues. During the growing season, the effects of grazing can be more significant. If a plant is grazed repeatedly in the early growing season, it may exhaust its energy without a chance to recover. Severe grazing just before seed is set can also be very harmful. Evaluating grazing impacts and recovery during

Overgrazing and Overrest

Overgrazing occurs when a severely grazed plant does not have time to recover before being grazed again. A plant that is grazed once or twice, then allowed to rest for the remainder of the growing season, is very likely to recover completely. If it is grazed repeatedly, it will have less time and reduced resources for recovery. The health of the plant depends on both its leaves and its roots, and an overgrazed plant tends to have shallower roots, weakening its ability to recover from subsequent grazing events or to withstand other disturbances such as drought. A downward spiral can result: less forage for cows, who then impact each plant more severely, leading to still less forage, and so on. Livestock, plants, soils, watersheds, wildlife, and ranchers all suffer when overgrazing occurs.

Note that the critical issue is *time.* The number of cattle in a pasture is important, too, but only because higher stocking rates make it less likely that a grazed plant will have time to recover. Lower stocking rates make it more likely. Moreover, what makes for overgrazing changes from year to year and season to season. In a good year, with more moisture, plants recover more quickly; in a drought they recover slowly. So even a lightly stocked pasture may be overgrazed in a very dry year, whereas a heavily stocked one might not experience overgrazing in a very wet year. This is why ranchers like Jim Winder and Roger Bowe (see **The Beck Land and Cattle Company,** p. 59 and **The Rafter F Cattle Company**, p. 45) speed up their rotations in wetter years and slow them down in dry years. *Control of timing is critical to avoid overgrazing.*

Kirk Gadzia indicates the space between perennial plants on grazed land (above) and ungrazed land (below). These areas are about fifteen yards apart. The ungrazed land has not been used in forty years. (Photos courtesy of Courtney White.)

Overrest is, for certain grass species at least, the opposite of overgrazing. It occurs when disturbance is absent for such a long time that the accumulated growth of past years prevents the plants from cycling enough energy to remain vital. The old leaves give the plants a gray tone; they shade out areas where new plants could otherwise germinate; root systems slowly contract. (See photo on p. 4.) Overrest can occur even in the presence of livestock, since decadent plants are not palatable and may be avoided.

In the long run, overrested areas are prone to a fate similar to overgrazed ones. Eventually, some disturbance will occur—a drought or a fire, for instance—and the weakened plants may be unable to recover, leading to more bare soil, erosion, etc. (The same risk attends forests where fire has been suppressed for too long.) In ecosystems adapted to disturbance, managers must negotiate carefully between overgrazing and overrest.

fact, ungrazed areas experienced higher mortality of black grama than moderately grazed areas *[50, 51]*.) During periods of good rainfall, on the other hand, recovery is possible even from rather heavy grazing impacts. As the saying goes, it's easy to be a good ranch manager in a wet year.

The problem, of course, is that rainfall is unpredictable and uncontrollable. Management must focus instead on things that can be managed. In the next chapter we will examine ways that management can indirectly influence the availability of moisture and nutrients, thereby minimizing the severity of drought periods. For now, the important point is that recovery must be allowed to happen. (See **Overgrazing and Overrest**, p. 31.)

Revegetated gully at Cuba mine site. (Photo courtesy of Courtney White.)

Conclusion

In this chapter we have considered the relation between a plant and a grazing animal: how the animal behaves in grazing and how the plant responds. We have seen that grazing is highly variable, and that its effects depend on timing, intensity, and frequency. Of course, no rancher can control exactly how each plant is grazed by each animal. But management can control the timing, intensity, and frequency of grazing at the pasture scale.

Before turning to management, we have to consider the cumulative, larger-scale effects of grazing: how it intersects with processes that occur across a landscape and, usually, over longer periods of time. Competition among plants, for example, occurs at very small scales (affecting individual plants) and much larger scales (affecting whole populations) simultaneously. Grazing rarely kills a plant directly, but it can tilt the competitive balance among different plant species, indirectly killing those that are most severely grazed *[6]*. These changes may be so slow as to escape notice, or they may take place quite rapidly following a major disturbance such as severe drought, flood, or fire. These processes are more difficult to study, and generally less well understood, than the direct effects of grazing. They require understanding of the ecological relationships among grazers, plants, soils, water, and energy.

THE EMPIRE RANCH
Sonoita, Arizona

"To keep things the same, you've got to change something."
--Empire Ranch Biological Assessment Team member

John Donaldson and his son, Mac, have managed the Empire Ranch since 1975. The ranch comprises about 72,000 acres, divided roughly equally between Bureau of Land Management and Arizona State Land Department ownership. The ranch is located between 4,300 and 5,200 feet in elevation and receives an average of about thirteen inches of precipitation per year.

The BLM bought the Empire in 1988 for conservation purposes. Plans to subdivide the ranch's deeded acres had been floating around for two decades, potentially threatening to deplete the headwaters of Cienega Creek, a perennial stream with a rich assemblage of riparian-dependent rare and endangered species. The BLM honored, then extended, the

Donaldsons' existing leases to graze the ranch.

John Donaldson had owned the Tortuga Ranch, southwest of Tucson, since 1952, and the lessons he learned there informed his management on the Empire. He had learned, for example, that the amount of forage produced by the range varies widely from year to year, depending on when, where, and how it rained. Pastures that received run-off from higher in the watershed produced different forage, and had different soils, from the adjacent mountain pastures. Donaldson used spreader dams to distribute run-off across the bottomlands, producing a rich crop of summer forage that allowed him to rest the mountains throughout the growing season. In good years, he brought in additional

Alkali Sacaton

33

stockers to use the forage, while in bad years he cut back the herd significantly.

The Empire is higher and wetter than the Tortuga, and conditions are somewhat different. But the principles involved are basically the same. John and Mac call their management "flexible grazing," because it aims to adapt to the constantly changing range conditions. Their herd ranges in size from 600 to 1,400 head (the official carrying capacity is 1,500). They run them as a group, rotating every two to four weeks throughout the summer growing season and less frequently in the dormant season. The size of the herd and the rotation vary according to forage availability.

The Donaldsons have divided the Empire's range into thirty-one pastures, based largely on the different ecological traits of the land. The old floodplain bottomlands, dominated by Sacaton, can produce as much as 5,000 pounds of forage per acre, so they are divided into much smaller pastures (they make up more than half the pastures, but less than four percent of the acres of the ranch). These are used primarily in the spring and summer, when the cows' needs are greatest (for breeding and lactation) and when the herd would be unlikely to utilize the rougher country in the uplands. This allows upland pastures to rest through most or all of the growing season every year. Pastures are evaluated before and after the growing season to determine how much forage is available: grasses, forbs, and browse each figure into the calculations.

As a publicly owned conser-

vation area, the Empire is subject to a great deal of scrutiny. In 1994, the Donaldsons and the BLM put together a Biological Planning Team, composed of representatives from the local community, the environmental community, and all the agencies with a stake in the ranch (including the Arizona Game and Fish Department, the Natural Resource Conservation Service, and the Fish and Wildlife Service, as well as the BLM and the Arizona State Land Department). The Team meets in the spring to discuss plans for the summer's grazing, and again in the fall to review results. They also resolve issues on a wide range of other topics: endangered species, riparian areas, hunting, recreation, fire, water development, and so forth. Extensive monitoring is done to document conditions and inform management; a large number of livestock exclosures have been created to provide a benchmark for evaluating the effects of grazing. The scientific data provide an objective lens for the Team to use in approaching contentious issues.

All told, the Empire is a model of sustainable, multiple-use management of public lands. Endangered species are thriving in and along the creek, in areas excluded from cattle and in areas that are grazed. Mountain bikers, horseback riders, hunters, birders, and campers all use the ranch in large numbers. (Indeed, recreation may soon become a more difficult issue than grazing for the Planning Team to manage.) And the Donaldsons' herd is prospering.

Chapter Three
The Spatial and Temporal Distribution of Water and Nutrients

"Since you're
human,
don't forget:
it's not people who
give
pure, sweet water
to plants--
it's the black-wet-
bland soil
does that..."
--*Makoto Ooka*

Understanding Grazing at Larger Scales

The Donaldsons' management of the Empire Ranch illustrates that grazing cannot be understood simply as an impact on individual plants. How plants respond has as much or more to do with larger conditions in the area: the other plants present, topography and soils, or whether it's a dry year or a wet one. The area in question may be as small as a hill slope or as large as an entire watershed. Although these conditions can vary widely from year to year, and they can sometimes change abruptly, they generally develop over many years' time. We must therefore expand the scale of our examination to encompass larger areas and longer periods of time.

From a practical point of view, management cannot control the grazing of individual plants. Decisions must be taken on larger scales: pastures or entire ranches. From an ecological point of view, the processes that influence plants operate across larger scales as well [6]. Different factors assume primary importance depending on the scale of analysis. Long-term, large-scale changes in vegetation, for example, are driven primarily by climate. Shorter-term changes may depend on discrete events, such as a fire, a flood, or a hard frost. On smaller spatial scales, the vegetation on opposite sides of the same hill may differ due to aspect; the competition between

Returning vegetation on Ogilvie Cattle Co. Ranch riparian area. (Photo courtesy of Courtney White.)

mentioned earlier, the advantage of focusing on ecological processes is that we avoid having to make assumptions about scale.

In the last chapter, we looked at a single grass plant over the course of one year. We observed that it grows when conditions are right. In this chapter, we ask what it means for conditions to be right. We are also concerned with the longer-term issue of whether that plant will reproduce successfully, such that the species persists after the plant dies. We have examined the stages leading up to seed production; now we consider the processes that determine if those seeds will germinate and grow to maturity.

two neighboring grass plants may be determined by the growth of a nearby tree, or the arrival of a particular kind of insect. In general, the smaller the scale (in space or time) of what you look at, the more particular factors you will need, in order to explain how it came into being.

The effects of grazing, like other ecological processes, are also scale-dependent. Moderate grazing has been shown to increase variability of plant composition if measured at a large spatial scale, but decrease it if measured at smaller scales. Heavy grazing, by contrast, reduced variability at all scales [37]. Two lessons may be drawn from this. First, there is no single "correct" scale for understanding the effects of grazing. Second, the greater the disturbance caused by grazing, the more likely that it will override other factors that also influence plants. As

The Importance of Water and Nutrients

Two ecological processes strongly determine the vigor and composition of vegetation, especially in arid and semiarid rangelands: the flow or cycling of water and nutrients. Put simply, the plants on a range—what they are and how well they are growing—are a reflection of these underlying ecological processes. The goal is to develop means of managing grazing for improved water and nutrient availability, in order to benefit all the organisms—including cattle and humans, plants, and wildlife—that depend on rangelands.

Plants require water, nutrients, and sunlight for growth. Sunlight is abundant in arid and semiarid regions, but small-scale variations can be important. The shade cast by trees, for instance, can inhibit seedling establishment and growth. Grass plants with large amounts of old foliage can shade their own growth points, slowing further growth. Finally, the presence of plants and litter has a strong effect on ground surface temperatures and evaporation rates. Bare ground is hotter, drier, more subject to temperature extremes, and less likely to permit germination of new plants. Moreover, bare ground is poor habitat for the microorganisms and insects that enhance nutrient cycling.

Water and nutrients are not static quantities: they increase and decrease, sometimes rapidly, and they move around. The issue is therefore not simply how much moisture or nutrients there are, but whether they are available to plants when they need them. A heavy rainfall that runs off quickly has a different effect than a longer, lighter rain, even if the overall amount of rainfall is the same. Large quantities of nutrients may be present in an area but unavailable to plants because they are fixed in a form that can't be used. A standing crop of dead plant matter, for example, must somehow return to the soil and decompose before it can help to nourish living plants.

In arid and semiarid regions, small changes in the availability of water and nutrients can have dramatic effects on vegetation. The nutrients contained in a cow's dung can significantly increase germination rates, for example. A small relief feature can capture extra run-off and allow a different community of vegetation to develop. The sensitivity of vegetation to water and nutrient availability is both a caution and an opportunity to management. Mistakes can be grave in their consequences, but small improvements can also ramify through the landscape and have significant beneficial effects. No one can control the rain, but management decisions can affect how

Figure 3. Where vegetation is dense, water flows are tortuous. Erosive energy is dissipated, and more water absorbs into the ground as it moves across the land. Source: Ludwig et al. 1997: 15. [68]

An example of an area on Sandia Pueblo with a poor water cycle. (Photo courtesy of Kirk Gadzia.)

much of the rain that does fall will benefit the local ecosystem.

The Water Cycle

Water is constantly cycling between the earth and the atmosphere. It falls as rain or snow. Some of it enters the ground, some of it runs downward toward the sea. Eventually it evaporates and returns to the atmosphere. Along the way, it may move through plants, animals, or aquifers. We are interested here in a portion of the overall cycle, beginning when water reaches the ground or vegetation and ending when it leaves the range in question.

Moisture is scarce in arid and semiarid areas by definition. In the western United States, precipitation is highly variable across the landscape and over time. The key issue is how much of the total precipitation is retained in the system and for how long, because this determines the *effectiveness* of the moisture: how much use it can

be put to by plants. A second, related issue is erosion: the potential for water to carry off topsoil and nutrients as it moves through the system. Where erosion is high, water retention tends to be low.

Vegetation strongly affects the distribution of water in space and time (see **The McNeils: Measuring Success in a New Way**, p. 43) *[106]*. In the absence of vegetation, water hits the ground surface at a high rate of speed. The impact dislodges fine soil particles, which then clog the pores of the soil, greatly reducing infiltration. This, in turn, accelerates erosional processes. Soil particles attach to the water molecules and are transported downhill in run-off, reducing the quality of the soil that remains. In extreme cases, a thin crusty surface ("capping") develops which encourages run-off and inhibits plant establishment, reinforcing the cycle of degradation (see **The Soil Surface: Litter, Capping, and Biological Crusts**, p. 55).

If a raindrop hits plants or litter, on the other hand, the impact on the soil is greatly diminished. Even a thin cover of litter will protect soil from capping and reduce erosion. Live plants intercept water both from the sky and running off from higher ground. By slowing its progress, the plants diminish the water's erosive power (Figure 3, p. 37). Studies indicate that small increases in the basal cover of plants can dramatically

Biodiversity and Resilience

Biological diversity, or biodiversity for short, may seem like a threatening term to many ranchers. It is, after all, the watchword of many environmental groups, a term with mysterious meaning and grand, almost divine significance. This is unfortunate, because although it is sometimes used as a political weapon against public lands grazing, biodiversity need not be a threat to ranchers at all. Nor is grazing a threat to biodiversity [100], especially compared to urbanization [35, 47]. Indeed, unlike most of modern agriculture, range livestock production *needs* biodiversity, because greater diversity gives rangelands greater resilience to variable conditions and to disturbances, including grazing.

The precise scientific definition of biodiversity *is* complex, and there are countless aspects of it that remain highly mysterious to biologists of all kinds. But for present purposes, it can be understood as the variety of biological organisms (or species) present in any given area or ecosystem. Each species has particular requirements to survive: a certain range of climatic conditions, energy sources, etc. Where conditions are highly variable, as they are in Southwestern rangelands, high biodiversity increases the likelihood that some species will thrive no matter what conditions prevail at any particular time. To put it the other way around, high biodiversity makes it less likely that all the species present will decline simultaneously during a time of severe stress or disturbance. A diversity of vegetation makes the range as a whole more *resilient*: capable of recovering from whatever stresses or disturbances occur.

This should be familiar to most ranchers. Different forage species are at their most palatable at different times of the year. Ideally, your range has a sufficient variety of plants to provide nutritious forage throughout the year. (Most likely, forage value peaks at a particular time, depending on the seasonality of your best forage plants—Sid Goodloe's oak brush, for example.) A diverse assemblage of perennial grasses provides more reliable year-around forage and is better able to withstand fluctuations in rainfall, temperature, etc. Imagine if you had only one or two types of plants on your ranch: could your cattle make it through the year? a drought?

decrease rates of run-off.

Plants also help to increase the infiltration of water into the soil. The leaves of grass plants catch water and deliver it to the base of the plant, where it is unlikely to disrupt the soil upon impact. Roots open pores in the ground and support communities of insects, fungi, and bacteria that create cavities and tunnels for water to pass through. Studies have found that the presence of termites, for example, dramatically increases water infiltration [32]. Without plants to feed on, termites disappear and the soil becomes more compact and impermeable. The difference is especially pronounced when rainfall is torrential, as in Southwestern summer monsoons.

"The more water that is retained in the soil, the more resilient the system will be to extremes of rainfall or drought."

The type of plants present also affects the water cycle, at two levels. Above ground, trees such as juniper have higher rates of interception loss (evaporation of water directly from the surface of the plant) and transpiration (water vapor loss through plant tissues) than do grasses. Below ground, woody species tend to utilize water from a greater area and volume of soil, and for a greater proportion of the year, than do grasses *[102]*. As Sid Goodloe and other ranchers have learned from experience, rangelands dominated by grass capture a lot more water than areas dominated by shrubs and trees do.

The more water that is retained in the soil, the more resilient the system will be to extremes of rainfall or drought. Floods will be less damaging, because the vegetation and soil will slow and diminish the overall amount of run-off. Droughts will be less damaging, because the water in the ground will prolong the life of plants during dry periods. A properly functioning watershed can make the difference between plants surviving a drought or not.

As the water in the ground increases, it may eventually add to the local water table. Sid Goodloe's Carrizo Valley Creek illustrates improved watershed functioning attributable to vegetation changes. Studies have found that converting shrublands to grasslands will increase water yield in areas receiving more than eighteen inches of precipitation per year *[102]*. In drier areas, however, yields do not increase, because rates of evaporation from the soil are so high. Which is why ranchers at lower (i.e., drier) elevations of the Southwest have discovered that restoring grasses can cause surface stocktanks to cease filling: the water is captured in the soil, where it benefits plants and underground water supplies. Both scenarios illustrate the power of management to affect the distribution of water on rangelands.

The ideal distribution of water will vary depending on the landscape in question, but the goal can be expressed simply: *capture* as much of the rain that falls as possible, *retain* that water in the soil, so that it can be *safely released* to plants and downstream areas over time. This describes a watershed that is functioning properly, and its importance cannot be stated strongly enough. What the rain gauge tells you is only half the story—it's what happens after the rain comes down that will determine if it does any good for the plants on the range.

Roads and other man-made features of the landscape also have a strong effect on the spatial distribution of water. A road that traverses a slope may divert water from above and prevent it from reaching vegetation downslope, eventually causing a change in the plants growing there. Pavement will concentrate more water than normal in a ditch or other adjacent area. These things are simple and obvious enough, but their impacts on vegetation in areas where moisture is the key limiting factor can be far more dramatic than one might expect.

The importance of water distribution is illustrated most dramatically by riparian areas. These are places where water runs on in large quantities, concentrating its effectiveness in small areas. Generally speaking, riparian areas also receive nutrients from elsewhere, transported by the water. The combined effect of these processes is to make riparian areas significantly richer in the key factors for plant growth: water and nutrients. They are thus more dynamic, from an ecological point of view. Especially in the Southwest, riparian plant species are adapted to disturbance, particularly in the form of flooding. Taken together, these factors enable riparian areas to recover from disturbance more quickly than uplands, and to produce much larger volumes of forage. They are highly resilient, ecologically speaking. They are also key sites for range improvement, as we will see.

The Nutrient Cycle

The nutrient cycle is more difficult to see than the water cycle. It consists in the movement of nitrogen, phosphorus, and other minerals from the soil, through plants, and eventually back into the soil. Along the way, nutrients may be ingested by grazers, transported to another location and deposited in feces, or removed from the range

Erosion on Largo Creek. (Photo courtesy of Courtney White.)

when the animal is harvested for human consumption. Nutrients in plants also may fall to the ground as dead leaves or as ash from a fire. In most cases, nutrients are further broken down and made available to plants by decomposers: insects, fungi, bacteria, and invertebrates.

The more effectively the nutrient cycle functions, the more nutrients are available to support plant growth. Nitrogen availability can limit plant growth in desert ecosystems almost as much as water does, and in some cases perhaps more [44, 70]. Even small differences in available nutrients can affect what plants grow, if any, in an arid or semiarid environment. Scientists refer to this as "islands of fertility": small areas around the base of trees, for example, where nutrients concentrate and more plants grow [95, 96].

As noted earlier, decomposers are a key link in the nutrient cycle. Termites consume the majority of dead plant matter in Southwestern

[Above] Sid Goodloe looking for the presence of microbes. (Photo courtesy of Sid Goodloe.)
[Below] Cow patty. (Photo courtesy of Courtney White.)

deserts. Without their activity, much of the nutrients in dead plants would remain trapped in standing matter, unavailable to other plants. Eventually the nutrients would escape into the air through oxidation. Instead they are consumed by termites and move downward to the surface and subsurface of the ground. The termites are then consumed by predators like ants, who return the nutrients to the soil in their excrement. Research in the Chihuahuan desert suggests that the cycling of nitrogen is more important than new inputs of nitrogen from rainfall, and that a significant fraction of the total nitrogen cycled passes through termites and their predators [70].

In the passage of nutrients from the soil to plants, other organisms also play roles. Tiny fungi form symbiotic relationships with plant roots, assisting in the uptake of water and nutrients from the surrounding soil. These mycorrhizal fungi help to increase the survival of seedlings and the growth of mature plants. But they exist only in relation to certain kinds of plants, including grasses and perennial forbs. If their host plants disappear, so do they, and in their absence, other types of plants (shrubs and annual forbs, for example) will have a greater chance of establishing [27].

If decomposers are active, manure patties will break down and disappear from view quickly, usually within a year. Insects will be visible when you break open a dried patty. The fine filaments of mycorrhizal fungi will be just barely visible in a handful of topsoil. Termite casings will be found near the base of some plants. These are indicators that decomposition is occurring at appropriate rates. They may seem insignificant, but decomposers are critical to the potential productivity of arid and semiarid rangelands [119].

Disturbances like grazing and fire play a role in the nutrient cycle by reducing the standing crop of old plant material and bringing it into contact with the ground, either as manure, ash, or by trampling. Like all disturbances, these can have positive or negative effects depending on timing, intensity, and fre-

The McNeils: Measuring Success in a New Way

Mike and Cathy McNeil's ranch in south-central Colorado has been in the family for more than a century. For the first ninety years, the ranch followed a fairly set pattern. In the summer, most of the cattle grazed on U.S. Forest Service land in the nearby San Juan Mountains, while the family worked cutting and stacking (or baling) hay from the native hay meadows down on the ranch. In the winter, the cattle fed at the ranch on the hay produced the previous summer. Mike's father, like his father before him, took pride in the fact that the McNeil Ranch put up the biggest haystacks in the valley, and neighbors looked to the McNeils for clues about when to get started on the hard summer's work of haying.

Following a drought in 1989, Mike and Cathy initiated a series of dramatic changes in their management, based on the principles of Allan Savory's Holistic Management. The drought had almost resulted in a cut on their Forest allotment, for which they were not prepared. As they scrutinized their operation, they began to realize that cutting so much hay no longer made sense, economically or otherwise. The costs of heavy equipment, fuel, and labor far outweighed the gains in nutritional quality of hay compared to simply leaving the grass where it grew. Haying was harder on the grass plants, too. With a modest investment in fences and water, they split their twelve pastures into twenty-five. They instituted a rotation and a breeding schedule based on the needs of the grasses, and they sold most of their haying equipment. Today they run more cattle on the same land, with lower operation costs and higher profits, and a lot less stress. Why work all summer to cut the hay, and all winter to feed it, when the cattle can do the job themselves?

The key to successful management, say Mike and Cathy, is good decision-making and planning. Change is always difficult, and one of the biggest obstacles they faced was the family tradition. How could they, the McNeils, *not* stack hay, when having the biggest, best haystacks in the valley had helped define the family's values and standing for three and a half generations?

One part of the answer is that, economically, Mike and Cathy couldn't afford to let traditional management continue unquestioned. A new measure of their management was needed, and they've found it. Instead of big haystacks, Mike and Cathy point at the ground. Look at the plant spacing, they say: it used to average two inches, now it's only one.

For more on the McNeil Ranch's management changes, see the Quivira Coalition Newsletter of February 2000, vol.3, no. 2.

quency. If heavy animal impact or a fire is followed by light, steady rain, the additional nutrients and sunlight may produce a thick growth of new vegetation. But a heavy rain, or severe drought, after such disturbance can result in tremendous erosion, carrying nutrients away.

The nutrient cycle is strongly affected by the water cycle, for better

Cut and piled hay at the McNeil Ranch. (Photo courtesy of Cathy McNeil.)

and for worse. Plants are the mechanism that enables the two cycles to reinforce each other. An area with good plant cover will retain more water and cycle more nutrients, allowing the plants to survive droughts better and to produce still more vegetation in good years. If the soil is hard and bare, on the other hand, less moisture penetrates into the ground, which dries out more quickly and makes plant growth more difficult, which in turn diminishes the amount of nutrients being cycled in the area. When considered over periods of several years, these reinforcing cycles are extremely important, especially in areas of low or erratic precipitation.

Conclusion

The processes that determine water and nutrient availability come together at the surface of the ground. If the soil is stable and the watershed is functioning properly, the potential for long-term sustainable production of forage is good. Chances are that the range will be able to recover from disturbances like drought and grazing. Soil loss by wind and water erosion, on the other hand, weakens the resilience of the system, making it vulnerable to disturbances. Productivity will gradually diminish, usually for a long time. Little wonder, then, that the Committee on Rangeland Classification of the National Academy of Sciences identified soil stability and watershed function as the first of three criteria for evaluating rangeland health. The other two? Integrity of nutrient cycles and energy flow, and the presence of functioning recovery mechanisms. Roger Bowe puts the matter more bluntly. "Bare ground," he says, "is the rancher's number one enemy."

THE RAFTER F CATTLE COMPANY
San Jon, New Mexico

"Bare ground is the rancher's number one emeny."
--Roger Bowe

The Rafter F Cattle Company has been in the Bowe family for four generations. Roger and Debby Bowe manage the ranch, which comprises 14,200 acres of private land and 800 acres of New Mexico State Land. The ranch is about 4,000 feet in elevation and receives an average of fifteen inches of precipitation per year.

Prior to 1985, the Bowes ran about eighteen head per section, in keeping with the recommended stocking rate for the area. Grazing was continuous year around, and the carrying capacity was in a long, slow decline. The cattle were evenly distributed across the ranch, but their impact was uneven: They tended to graze the flat mesa tops, where sandier soils supported a sod-bound mat of blue grama grass and

buffalo grass. They stayed out of the bottoms, where the soil has more clay and the vegetation was almost entirely tobosa grass. The cattle did not suffer from this arrangement, since the blue grama and buffalo grass were ample for their needs. But the plants were not vigorous. In Roger's view, the "top flats" were overgrazed because the sod never had a chance to recover from grazing and set seed. It had become a mat of low grasses. The tobosa bottoms, meanwhile, were overrested. The plants there had become senescent: coarse and grey in color.

Economic pressures compelled the Bowes to make changes to try to increase the productivity of the ranch. They attended a seminar in Holistic Management taught by Allan Savory. Then they sent Roger's

45

Side-oats Grama

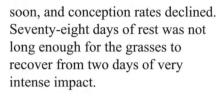
MONITORING RESULTS - BOWE RANCH SAN JON, NEW MEXICO USA						
NORTH CELL	1984	1986	1990	1991	1992	1993
% BARE GROUND	46	54	25	26	39	30
% LITTER	44	39	57	62	49	54
% BASAL COVER	8	7	18	17	17	16
% MATURE CAPPING	42	22	2	2	5	2
AVG. PLANT DISTANCE	1.8	0.86	.96	.70	.95	.69
SPECIES PERENNIAL GRASS	6	NA	17	17	17	18
LBS. BEEF PER ACRE	14	23	29	31	31	26
NET INCOME PER ACRE	5.84	8.00	19.4	18.4	22.5	NA
% BROOM SNAKEWEED	11	NA	1	1	1	1

Figure 4. Roger Bowe's Monitoring Results, over a nine-year period.

father to the same seminar in an effort to persuade him that overgrazing had more to do with timing than with the number of cattle on the ranch. Then they did exactly what Savory had told them *not* to do: built fences. Using wire salvaged from the area and their own labor, they divided the ranch into five grazing cells, each with eight pastures arrayed radially around a central water source. They installed waterlines and a few new wells to ensure that they would always have water where they needed it. They almost tripled the number of cattle, gathered them together, and commenced short-duration grazing, moving the herd every two days.

The new system encountered several problems at first. The cattle were not accustomed to moving so often or being in a herd, and they still didn't care for the coarse tobosa grass. The increased stocking rate was too much, too

soon, and conception rates declined. Seventy-eight days of rest was not long enough for the grasses to recover from two days of very intense impact.

The Bowes had installed monitoring transects to measure productivity, basal cover, vegetative composition and vigor, and soil surface cover (litter). When they analyzed the data after one year, they found that litter had declined by five percent. This was unexpected and caused them to make two changes. They cut the herd twenty percent, and they added twenty-two more pastures, bringing the total to sixty-two. (See photo on p. 47.) This allowed them to provide 122 days' rest between grazing periods. The herd was still much larger than it had been before 1985, large enough to compel the cattle to graze and trample the tobosa bottoms. This helped rejuvenate the plants there. In all, Roger reports that it took two or three years for the new system to prove itself.

Monitoring data collected since 1985 bears out the success of the Bowes' modified system. Bare ground has decreased by a third; litter cover has increased ten percent; basal cover has doubled. The average distance between plants has declined almost two-thirds, and snakeweed has declined by ninety percent. The number of perennial grass species on the ranch has tripled, from six to eighteen. Economically, the costs of production per pound of beef produced have dropped by over fifty percent, while net income per acre of land has more than tripled. The stocking rate is more than twice what it was before.

The benefits of the system can be seen in other ways, too. Numerous springs which had dried up before 1930 began to flow again in the 1990s. Water has returned to a hand-dug well which dried up in the 1950s. Stocktanks don't fill as readily as they used to, but the water they capture is now clear instead of muddy brown. Flood run-off is also clear, even after a torrential rain dropped eight inches in thirty-six hours in 1991. Sediment continues to run off of the neighboring ranch upstream, but it is captured on the Bowe Ranch bottomlands, enriching the soil there. The Bowes can gather their entire herd with two people, one on a motorcycle and one in a pickup, because the cattle have grown accustomed to moving often and in a herd.

The Bowes' management stands out not only for its ecological and economic results, but for the central role that careful monitoring has played in making decisions. Roger also monitors his cows, of course, using the system known as Body Condition Score (BCS). But he recognizes that monitoring the land itself must come first, and his monitoring program employs methods aimed at understanding basic ecological processes like the ones discussed in the last chapter. In this chapter, we discuss why monitoring is so important to managing the New Ranch.

ITEM:	1983	1990
BOWE RANCH RESULTS		
COST PER POUND OF BEEF		
FEED	.14	.09
REPAIRS	.02	.002
INTEREST	.07	.03
SUPPLIES	.03	.01
CHEMICALS	.01	0
VET & MED.	.02	.007
GAS & OIL	.02	.006
TAXES & INS	.02	.007
UTILITIES	.006	.003
LAND RTRN 3%	.25	.10
TOTAL	$.60	$.26

Figure 5. Bowe Ranch Cost per Pound of Beef.

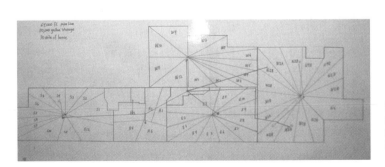

Rafter F pasture system. (Photo courtesy of Roger Bowe.)

Chapter Four
Thresholds and Monitoring

"The earth's vegetation is part of a web of life in which there are intimate and essential relations... Sometimes we have no choice but to disturb these relationships, but we should do so thoughtfully, with full awareness that what we do may have consequences remote in time and place."

--Rachel Carson

Understanding Rangeland Change

In Chapter One we examined the shortcomings of several conventional tools for managing grazing. The core problem concerned variability and scale. Arid and semiarid rangelands vary dramatically in vegetation and productivity, over both space and time. This variation limits the value of tools that assume either: 1) that larger areas are simply the sum of many smaller areas, or 2) that longer periods of time are simply the sum of shorter periods of time.

Chapters Two and Three described ecological processes: the growth of grasses, the flow of water, and the cycling of nutrients. These processes are interrelated and operate on a number of scales simultaneously, from individual plants up to watersheds, and from short periods (a growing season) to very long ones (decades, centuries, or even longer).

By focusing on the processes that produce forage, rather than just the forage itself, we begin to see all these scales at once. We understand grazing as a kind of disturbance, whose effects depend on timing, intensity, and frequency. Rangeland vegetation is adapted to disturbances—grazing, fire, flood, drought—and can recover from them within limits. But what are these limits? How can we observe and measure them? What happens if these limits are exceeded?

The timing, frequency, and intensity of grazing can be controlled, as we will see in the next chapter. But we need a larger framework to understand how these tools can be employed to preserve and increase range productivity over the longer term. The framework provided here comes from recent research that models how arid and semiarid rangelands change over space and time. More research is needed to refine these models, but they have already begun to be incorporated into the management of public rangelands.

Thresholds

Imagine a particle of dust on the ground as the wind gradually increases. For a while, the particle does not move. Then, at some point the wind attains enough speed to lift the particle off the ground and carry it away.

The relationship between wind speed and lifting the dust particle is not linear. Say we measured the wind and the height of the particle and found that, at twenty miles per hour, the wind lifted the dust twenty feet. It does not follow that each m.p.h. of wind lifted the particle one foot. The first nineteen miles per hour had no effect at all. Then, at twenty m.p.h., a *threshold* was crossed and the dust rose.

Thresholds are common in nature. Some of them are well known: water turns to ice at 32 degrees Fahrenheit, and to vapor at 212 degrees. Others are much harder to define. A wildfire may cross a threshold of heat, fuel, and oxygen beyond which it behaves

very differently— crowning out in the tree- tops, for ex- ample, instead of burn- ing along the ground. The key point is that change is not linear but subject to abrupt shifts. The more complicated the system under observation, the more difficult it is to pinpoint just what causes these shifts. In theory, whenever change is non-linear across scales, some threshold must exist to explain it.

In recent decades the idea of thresholds has been applied to the study of arid and semiarid rangelands *[21, 36, 66, 117]*. Take for example the shift from grasslands to shrublands in the Southwestern United States *[69]*. Ecologists recognize several contributing factors: overgrazing, fire suppres-

Rio Puerco near Cuba, New Mexico. (Photo courtesy of Courtney White.)

sion, drought, a change in seasonal rainfall patterns, and an increase in atmospheric CO_2 levels. There seems to be no way to isolate a single one as *the* cause; different combinations may have occurred in different places. In any case, once the shift to shrublands occurs, grasslands do not reappear on their own. Some threshold is crossed, beyond which the change becomes self-reinforcing. Once mesquites reach a certain density, for example, abrupt decreases in grass cover and increases in erosion have been observed. Once the grasses decrease below some amount of cover, there isn't enough fuel for a fire. Without fire, the mesquites persist and dominate further. What was once a grassland is now a shrubland, and will remain a shrubland until some drastic disturbance occurs, naturally or otherwise *[75]*. Resting the land

by excluding livestock does nothing to restore grasses.

State and Transition Models

Scientists have introduced a model of rangeland ecosystems, called the "state and transition" model, to account for thresholds of change over time. "States" are relatively stable associations of vegetation that may occur in a given area; "transitions" are the pathways of change across thresholds from one state to another *[117, 118]*. To date, these models remain largely qualitative and somewhat hypothetical.

A state and transition model for lowland sites in the Chihuahuan Desert Grassland is presented in Figure 6. It depicts three major states: grassland, grassland-shrubland, and shrubland. Within each state are a number of vegetation associations, defined by one or two

Figure 6. A state and transition model for an ecological site in the Chihuahuan Desert Grassland (working draft, courtesy of Dr. Brandon Bestelmeyer, Jornada Experimental Range). The solid arrows represent transitions that are known from data collected at the Jornada Experimental Range; the dashed arrows are hypothesized transitions. The vertical, dashed lines are thresholds that divide groups of relatively stable states.

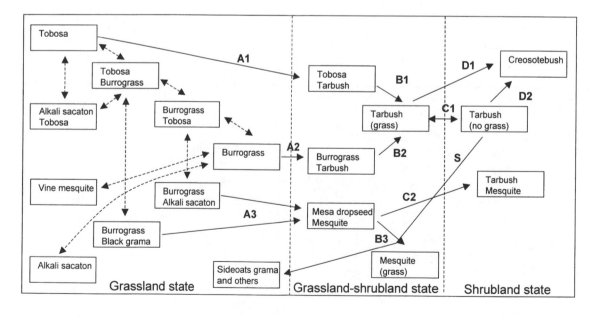

dominant species. Eleven transitional pathways are identified from data; others are hypothesized. The critical transitions are those that cross from one state to another— that is, across a threshold.

The model differs from earlier, successional models in two important respects. First, it recognizes several possible sequences of change, rather than a single continuum of seral stages. Second, it recognizes thresholds of change that are induced by disturbance and not easily reversed, even in the absence of grazing. Most of the transitions are associated with disturbances such as grazing, drought, and fire. State and transition models have recently been incorporated into the management protocols of the Natural Resource Conservation Service *[42]*.

Patches: Models from Australia

Other scientists, working in Australia, have attempted to model variability across space in a way that resembles the state and transition models of change over time *[68]*. They describe arid and semiarid landscapes as mosaics of bare ground and vegetation of various kinds. These "patches" interact with each other to distribute scarce

Erosion, pedestaling. (Photo courtesy of Kirk Gadzia.)

resources such as water and nutrients. A patch of bare ground, for example, sheds water downhill. The water picks up litter and sediment and deposits it someplace else, where it encounters vegetation or flat ground. The receiving patch thus accumulates more resources, enabling more or different vegetation to grow. In this model, the thresholds are spatial ones that can be measured in terms of moisture, nutrients, or microclimatic conditions like soil temperature. Patches, like states, tend to be self-reinforcing. They can of course change, due to disturbances like fire or grazing, flood, or drought.

In theory, these two new models can be combined. Every "state" can be seen as a mosaic of patches interacting with each other. Each patch is characterized by differentials of water and nutrient availability that determine what grows there. Transitions occur when the relations among patches change, pushing the system as a whole across a threshold of change. Heavy grazing during a drought, for instance, might eliminate many small patches of grass, causing a

Healing riparian area on Rafter F Ranch. (Photo courtesy of Roger Bowe.)

hillside to become one large patch of bare ground. This leads to increased run-off rates, concentrating water and nutrients in another area, perhaps many miles downstream. The hillside may not recover for many years, having lost the ability to retain moisture and nutrients needed for plant establishment.

The idea of thresholds helps to explain why degraded rangelands have not recovered with lighter grazing or even with complete exclusion of livestock. But change can also occur towards greater productivity and better ecological functioning. If good summer rains occur in two consecutive years, for example, perennial grasses can germinate in large numbers and compete successfully with annuals. Conversely, winter drought can stress undesirable species like burroweed more severely than grasses, creating a management opportunity.

The patch model provides a way to think about these thresholds of desirable change. Consider Sid Goodloe's Carrizo Creek, for example, or Roger Bowe's old springs. By increasing grass cover in the surrounding uplands, Goodloe and Bowe increased water retention in their watersheds. The water gradually accumulated and replenished the water tables in lower areas. At some threshold, the springs and the creek returned.

Riparian areas are the most productive parts of arid and semiarid landscapes because they receive water and nutrients from the uplands. One can expect vegetation to establish in riparian areas more quickly and reliably than anywhere else. Once a riparian area is well vegetated, moreover, it captures water and nutrients and retains them in the local area. These benefits can then spread outward: a rising water table can benefit nearby vegetation; the corridor of thick vegetation can expand; uplands can benefit by management changes made possible by the greater forage production in the riparian area. It is the opposite of the vicious cycle of nutrient and water loss described in the previous chapter: a positive feed-back loop, once established, can result in compounding ecological improvement.

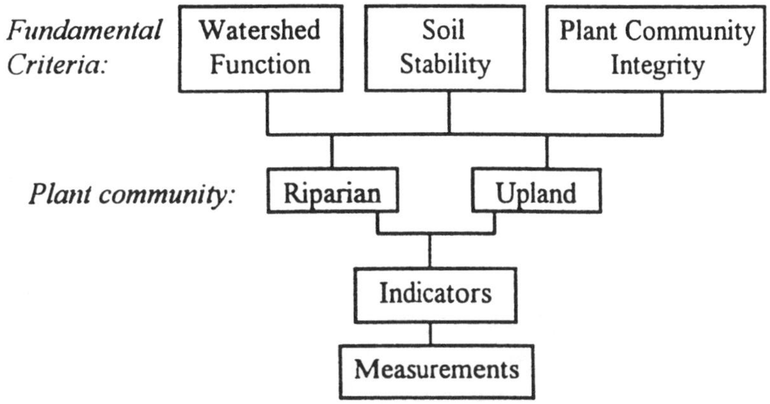

Fig. 7   Relationship between fundamental criteria, indicators and measurements for riparian and upland communities. [62]

The high degree of variability in arid and semiarid rangelands, combined with the issue of thresholds, makes management a very difficult challenge. The same grazing pressure can have little effect in a year of good rainfall, but cause lasting damage during a drought. It is much easier to prevent an area from crossing a threshold—from grassland to shrubland, for example—than it is to reverse the change after it has occurred. But science has not yet learned to predict exactly where these thresholds are. There are too many variables to consider all at once. How can management proceed?

Monitoring

The ecological processes discussed in earlier chapters are difficult to observe or measure directly. Most of a grass plant is below the ground, in the root system. Nutrients like nitrogen and phosphorus are invisible to the eye. You can look during a rainstorm to see if water is running off or soil is eroding, but most of the time water is moving under ground, evaporating into the air, or being used by plants in ways that aren't immediately observable.

Monitoring is a way of measuring ecological processes indirectly. The processes themselves cannot be observed, but *indicators* of the processes can be observed and measured (Figure 7). Litter cover, for example, is an indicator of the nutrient cycle, because for nutrients to cycle, organic material must be produced and then returned to the soil for decomposition. By monitoring litter cover over time, we learn valuable information about the functioning of the nutrient cycle, and, by extension, about the productivity of the land being monitored. Recall that Roger Bowe modified his new

Restoring Riparian Areas

Controlling the timing, intensity, and frequency of grazing is important on all rangelands, but the results of management are most apparent in riparian areas, where water and nutrients are more abundant than in the surrounding uplands. Jim Winder's Macho Creek is but one of numerous examples of riparian restoration through better control of grazing. (See photos on p. 56.)

Under continuous, year-round grazing, cattle tended to overutilize the riparian area, where forage, water, and shade were relatively abundant. As a result, plants were grazed repeatedly, with little time to rest. Over time, Macho Creek became little more than a depression in the range. During floods—as in the photo—the water was muddy with sediment. At other times, the creek was completely dry.

Jim's cattle still graze Macho Creek, but the timing of the grazing has been carefully controlled for the last fourteen years. Grazing occurs mostly in the dormant season, and only for very short periods of time, giving the plants ample time to recover. The resulting change has been dramatic, as the photos illustrate. Riparian trees have established and grown, and the creek has returned to clear, perennial flow. Forage production has also increased. In fact, Jim's cattle harvest ten times as much forage from Macho Creek than before, but with far less impact on the plants. Just upstream, where a similar management change has been implemented in a collaborative effort by the permittee, the State Land Office, the Quivira Coalition, the Jornada Experimental Range, and HawksAloft, monitoring has documented increases in both forage and songbird abundance and diversity.

These results are not exceptional. On Date Creek, in Arizona, rancher Phil Knight has restored an amazing cottonwood-willow forest (see photo above) simply by limiting grazing to

the winter, dormant season. (Before photo on left. [Photos courtesy of Dan Dagget.]) There are other examples from elsewhere in the Southwest *[15]* and the arid and semiarid West *[33, 64]*. Riparian areas in arid and semiarid regions are extremely important for wildlife, watershed functioning, and forage production. Fortunately, they can restore themselves fairly quickly given greater control over the timing, intensity, and frequency of grazing.

The Soil Surface: Litter, Capping, and Biological Crusts

Especially in arid and semiarid areas, the condition of the soil surface is critical to water and nutrient cycling. It is here that all the components needed for life come together: sunlight, water, minerals, air, plants. And it is here that they can come apart, under extreme natural conditions and/or poor management.

Litter—the bits and pieces of old plants that fall to the ground—is far more important than it appears. Not only does it represent important organic material for building up minerals in the soil, it also protects the soil from wind and water erosion. By absorbing the impact of raindrops, especially in heavy rainfall events, litter prevents soil particles from being dislodged and dispersed. Of course, living plants do this too, but in most arid and semiarid settings there isn't enough water to support a dense cover of living plants. Litter helps to fill in the gaps.

The importance of litter is illustrated by what happens where it's absent: Capping begins to develop. Raindrop impact separates fine soil particles, which then collect in soil pores, clogging them up. The soil surface hardens, gradually becoming impermeable to water and air. Plants cannot establish, because seeds cannot germinate. Without plants, there are no roots or insects to open up new pores in the soil. In certain soil types, the capping can become an inch thick and as hard as a tennis court. Water runs off quickly, and wind easily picks up small soil particles and any litter that arrives on site and carries them away. Serious capping represents the crossing of an ecological threshold: The cycle is self-reinforcing until some disturbance can break the capping and new plants can colonize the area.

Capping. (Photo courtesy of Kirk Gadzia.)

At the other extreme, and not to be confused with capping, are biological crusts (also known as cryptogamic, microphytic, or microbiotic crusts). These are crusts formed by microorganisms and bryophytes—mosses, lichens, algae, and cyanobacteria—interacting with the top few millimeters of the soil. In arid and semiarid areas, biological crusts play important ecological roles, somewhat similar to the role of plants: they stabilize soils against erosion. Biological crusts also assist in mineral nutrient cycling and can increase water infiltration and fix atmospheric nitrogen, making it available to plants. Biological crusts can thus help to bring an area back across the threshold, by creating conditions favorable to plant germination and insect activity [31].

Biological crusts are capable of withstanding severe droughts, but they are extremely vulnerable to physical disturbance. Fires, vehicles, livestock, and even human feet can damage crusts, especially when they are dried out [8, 90]. Recovery is slow: seven to twenty years or more, depending on conditions and the make-up of the crusts themselves [13, 61]. Research on biological crusts is active, and a great deal remains to be understood. It may be that some landscapes can support biological crusts but little more than that, in which case livestock grazing is effectively impossible. On the other hand, crusts may be interim states, which will gradually change as grasses establish and develop.

for signs of erosion, because the way water moves when it hits the ground is critical to the cycle as a whole. Roger Bowe stresses the importance of looking *down* at the land. If you look across it, you'll see lots of grass even where bare ground is more than fifty percent of the surface (see **The Soil Surface: Litter, Capping, and Biological Crusts**, p. 55).

Before (1986, above) and after (1993, below) a change in grazing management on Macho Creek. (Photos courtesy of Jim Winder.)

grazing system when his monitoring detected a five percent drop in litter cover. He would not have even noticed this change without a strong monitoring program.

Similarly, the water cycle can be monitored by measuring the amount of bare ground and looking

In a sense, every rancher monitors ecological processes already, by observing the condition of cattle or the water level in stocktanks, for example. These too are indicators: indirect reflections of vegetation or watershed conditions. The information they give is important to management. The trouble is that they are further removed from basic ecological processes than ground cover and vegetation. The cattle lose weight only after the grasses have declined; the stocktank fills with sediment (or blows out in a flood) only after the watershed has lost its capacity to retain moisture. You might say that these indicators are *too* indirect; the lag time may be too long to allow for effective management intervention, especially

where conditions are highly variable and subject to thresholds of change. Visual evaluation is also imprecise and subject to distortion.

Monitoring programs can be designed to measure almost anything, to almost any degree of precision. They can be as simple as a series of fixed points where you take photographs every year. Often they are more labor-intensive and require several years of committed effort to yield their full benefit in improved information. For these reasons, it is very important to choose one's monitoring objectives carefully, paying close attention to particular circumstances and needs. Time invested in good design can dramatically increase the efficiency and utility of monitoring (see **Designing a Monitoring System,** p. 58).

Above all, monitoring must be: 1) done consistently, year after year; 2) practicable—that is, not too time-consuming or difficult; and 3) related to management goals and activities. If it is not consistent, the data will be poor and perhaps reveal nothing. If it is not practicable, it becomes a nuisance which will either be avoided altogether or done poorly. And if it is not related to management, then the whole program may be little more than an academic exercise.

The point of monitoring is simple: it provides feedback that is more timely and objective than informal observation can ever be. Monitoring data can reveal the effects of management decisions

Monitoring. (Photo courtesy of Kris Havstad.)

well before they are apparent to the naked eye, greatly increasing one's ability to avoid lasting damage and to encourage range improvement. Every manager learns from experience, but good monitoring allows that learning to happen more quickly and systematically.

These days, monitoring data are also important for another reason, especially for ranchers who use public lands. They provide a documented record of range conditions and trends, based on objective, quantifiable measurement. Such a record is powerful testimony to the quality of management if you wind up in a Forest Service office or a courtroom facing criticisms from agency officials or environmentalists. Given the frequency of such disputes, it's fair to say that monitoring is no longer an optional exercise. It's a cost of doing business.

Designing a Monitoring Program

It is extremely important to design your monitoring program well, and to get professional assistance if necessary. Poorly designed monitoring will yield information that is either of poor quality or irrelevant to your management—either way, it will not be a good use of valuable time and resources.

How to design a monitoring program is addressed in the new *Monitoring Manual for Grassland, Shrubland and Savanna Ecosystems* recently developed by scientists at the Jornada Experimental Range in Las Cruces, New Mexico *[62]*. The manual provides clear, step-by-step guidelines for designing and implementing monitoring for a variety of objectives on rangelands. The Quivira Coalition, in partnership with the JER, offers workshops to train people in the protocol of the manual.

What you monitor and how you monitor depend on your management goals, the resource issues confronting you, and the amount of time and money you can afford to devote to it. Your monitoring program should *detect changes of importance to your goals* and *help you evaluate management decisions*. The Jornada protocol distinguishes four levels of monitoring, ranging from simple to complex:

● Level 1 monitoring is qualitative and descriptive: a simple record of what the range looks like. Fixed-point photographs, taken at the same time every year, are the best way to do this kind of monitoring.

● Level 2 monitoring provides feedback to management, combining Level 1 methods with records of utilization rates, stocking levels, dates of pasture rotations, and so forth. The fenceline contrast shown on p. 24, combined with the grazing information in the caption, is a simple example of what this might look like for one year. Monitoring the dates and amounts of precipitation is another important level 2 monitoring activity.

● Level 3 monitoring is quantitative and requires a certain amount of training. The vegetation transects employed by the Natural Resources Conservation Service are an example. The new Jornada protocol supplements vegetation data with monitoring for soil and watershed conditions, which will become more important to ranchers in the near future due to provisions of the Clean Water Act relating to rangelands. Level 3 monitoring provides information relevant to the ecological processes and functioning of the range.

● Level 4 monitoring is the most technical and specialized, and addresses specific resource issues such as endangered species. The program in place on the U Bar Ranch is an example (see **The Ogilvie Cattle Company and the U Bar Ranch**, p. 19).

At the very least, every ranch should have some Level 1 and Level 2 monitoring in place, to document conditions and management from year to year. It doesn't take much time or money, anyone can do it, and over time, you'll be surprised how much information can accumulate in a photo album and a notebook.

THE BECK LAND AND CATTLE COMPANY
Nutt, New Mexico

Jim Winder is owner and manager of the Beck Land and Cattle Company, located in south-western New Mexico. His two ranches comprise about 9,000 acres of private land, 24,000 acres of state land, and 40,000 acres of BLM land. Elevations range from 4,200 to 6,200 feet and precipitation averages about ten inches per year. Jim is a co-founder of the Quivira Coalition, and his experiences helped to inspire this handbook.

The ranch at Nutt has been in Jim's family for four generations. Thirteen years ago, Jim launched a rotational grazing system, using two-strand electric fences to divide the ranch into sixty-six pastures. Prior to that time, the ranch had had only three pastures, and the cattle had spent every summer in the same one. Now, Jim moves his cattle every one to three days throughout the growing season. Moves are planned so that no pasture is grazed at the same time from one year to the next. Riparian pastures are grazed predominantly in the dormant season and only for very short periods of time.

The range has responded dramatically to rotational grazing management. The diversity of grasses has increased on upland pastures, and prime forage species like bluestem are coming back. The Macho Creek riparian corridor has changed from a sandy trench to a densely vegetated ephemeral stream, and it now supports more than ten

Little Bluestem

Grass growing in a cow hoof print. (Photo courtesy of Jim Winder.)

to this as "dormant-based grazing," because it treats dormant grasses as the key forage base for planning purposes. In January and February, plans are adjusted depending on winter rains: a wet winter will produce a large crop of spring forbs that are highly nutritious for cattle. A dry winter means the forbs will not be coming and management will have to adjust. Around mid-March, Jim measures the spring forb crop, again in ADAs. Further adjustments are made at the end of July, depending on whether the summer rains have begun or not.

Jim stresses the importance of making stocking decisions early. He plans on the assumption that drought is a common occurrence in the Chihuahuan desert: five years out of ten will see less than average rainfall and two years in ten will be severely dry. By destocking at the first indication of drought, Jim minimizes the chance that drastic cuts will be necessary later on: the smaller the herd, the less quickly it will exhaust the supply of available forage. He keeps a combined herd of around sixty percent mother cows and forty percent stockers, so that he can destock easily if necessary by

times as much grazing as it did before (see photos, p. 56). Smaller gullies are also recovering, with cut banks becoming less steep and vegetation taking hold. The ranch carries twice as many cattle as before and about fifty percent more than the official carrying capacity for the area.

Jim's management requires careful planning ahead of time, as well as ongoing monitoring and flexibility to cope with changing conditions. At the end of the growing season, in October, Jim examines the forage that has grown and calculates how much grazing it will support. He does this in terms of animal-days per acre, or ADAs. The grazing plan for the coming year is based on these numbers. This way stocking decisions are made after the summer grasses have grown rather than before. Jim refers selling stockers.

It might seem like Jim's management would require a lot more work, with all the fencing and moving of cattle. Once established, however, the opposite is the case: the cost of labor per animal is less now than it was before. Jim points out that he always knows exactly where his cattle are, and he can see them all in fifteen minutes. The cattle are accustomed to frequent moves, and they cooperate readily because they have learned that fresh feed awaits them. Jim opens a gate, blows a whistle, and with some help from his dogs, moves the entire herd in less than half an hour. He can count them as they pass through the gate and watch for any problems. The cattle are more docile than they used to be, which cuts down on labor time and allows Jim to keep far fewer horses than before. And because they stay in a herd rather than dispersing, the cattle are better able to protect themselves against predators: Jim has lost only two calves to predators over the last thirteen years.

Jim likens all the fences to training wheels, which he needed at first but could now do without. His cattle have little inclination to break through them, since they never experience a shortage of feed. It's not the fences but the planning, the constant evaluation of conditions, and the flexibility that make his system work, he says. Cattle can be managed by controlling the supply of water, the location of mineral blocks, or by herding them with dogs (see **Herding**, p. 64).

Jim pays as much attention to the ground as he does to his cattle. Everywhere he goes on the ranch he looks for signs of the land's health. A key indicator of this, he feels, is in the soil itself: the fungi and termites and other decomposers that break down plant material and cycle nutrients back into the soil. He looks for insects in his cows' manure, and for termite casings at the base of plants. He notes the presence of wildlife scat or tracks—anything that might tell him something about how the range system is working or not working.

Jim considers himself a natural resource manager as much as a rancher. He reads articles from ecology journals and has consulted at length with scientists at the Jornada Experimental Range in Las Cruces. He devotes considerable time to working with conservation organizations, and he welcomes hundreds of visitors every year to tour his ranch and discuss rangeland health. While successful management has greatly improved his bottom line (and relations with his banker), Jim's philosophy subordinates economic returns to the needs of a healthy ecosystem. He predicts that, in time, ranchers will be paid as much for protecting watersheds, wildlife habitat, and biological diversity as for producing food.

Chapter Five

New Ranch Management

The Tools: Disturbance and Rest

The preceding chapters have outlined a scientifically informed framework that helps explain the successes of a handful of progressively managed ranches. By controlling the timing, intensity, and frequency of grazing, the New Ranch ensures that rangelands recover from the disturbance that grazing inevitably causes. And by focusing on the ecological processes that sustain range productivity, the New Ranch works to enhance and restore habitat for wildlife, proper functioning of watersheds, and—not least—economic vitality for the ranch operation.

It should be clear, however, that the practices of these ranchers do not constitute "scientific proof" of any single management program. Many things about arid and semiarid rangelands remain to be deciphered by scientific research. Sid Goodloe, David Ogilvie, John and Mac Donaldson, Roger Bowe, and Jim Winder have all adapted their management over time, taking risks and learning from their mistakes. They have combined scientific insights with personal observations, general principles with particular circumstances. This commitment to learn from the land, to focus as much on what we do not know as on what we do, is perhaps the single clearest lesson we can take from their experiences.

Now it is time to examine how this framework can be trans-

lated into management practices on the ground. Two primary tools are available: disturbance and rest. Some disturbances can be manipulated, like grazing and (to some degree) fire. Others, like drought and flood, are largely beyond the manager's control. The central principles of New Ranch management are to use the tools skillfully (control grazing and rest) and to plan for the disturbances that cannot be controlled. By exercising greater control over grazing pressure, and planning one's management to adapt to changing conditions, the New Ranch achieves sustainability, both economic and ecological.

Controlling the Timing, Intensity, and Frequency of Grazing

We have seen that grazing is a disturbance which, like other disturbances, may be good, bad, or indifferent in its impacts on rangelands. These impacts depend on when the disturbance occurs, how severe it is, and how soon it recurs. Hence the importance of controlling the timing, intensity, and frequency of grazing pressure.

Intensity. Intensity refers to how much biomass is removed from a plant by livestock. It measures the percentage of net primary production that is channeled into herbivores rather than consumed by fire, oxidation, or decomposers.

Intensity is a function of three variables: the number of animal units in a pasture, the length of time they are there, and the size

of the pasture. To manage intensity, therefore, requires a tool with three components: one for animals, one for time, and one for area. Animal-unit-months, or AUMs, is inadequate for this, because it has only two components: one for animals and one for time. Its time component, moreover, is rather gross: a month is not very precise. (This is especially true when one considers that AUMs were originally derived by dividing annual carrying capacity measurements by twelve to suit the management of seasonal grazing in Forest Service allotments.) Another conventional tool, stocking rates, also has only two components: one for animals and one for area. Head per section, or acres per head, takes no account of time. Utilization rates—which superficially resemble intensity—have none of the three components. A certain utilization rate may be a good goal for management, but it is not a practical tool. Something else is necessary to translate the goal into a management strategy.

Animal-days per acre, or ADAs, contains all three components necessary to measure and manage intensity. Adjustment must be made for the class of livestock being grazed. Roger Bowe calculates a mother cow as one animal unit, a cow with calf as 1.5 animal units, and a weaned calf as 0.7 animal units. Once this adjustment is made, animal-days per acre is exactly what it says: animal units, multiplied by days in the pasture, divided by the size of the pasture in acres. See **Using ADAs to Control Grazing**

"By exercising greater control over grazing pressure, and planning one's management to adapt to changing conditions, the New Ranch achieves sustainability, both economic and ecological."

Herding

Low-stress livestock management (herding) clinic at Ghost Ranch, May 2000. (Photo courtesy of Courtney White.)

On the West Elk allotment of the Gunnison National Forest in southwestern Colorado, six ranching families have revived the ancient practice of herding, updated with new ideas on planned grazing. The results have been positive all around: for the Forest (including the West Elk Wilderness Area), for the forage species, for the cattle, and for the ranchers' quality of life and economic returns.

The six ranching families pooled their cattle into a single herd for the summer grazing season beginning in 1981. It's more economical to tend and monitor one large herd (over 1,000 cow-calf pairs) than six smaller ones, and the arrangement afforded a much larger area to work with (90,000 acres). The families hire a full-time herder, or rotate the job among themselves, with additional riders available for big moves. The herd uses thirty grazing units each summer, moving every three to twenty days. The schedule is carefully planned ahead of time, but still flexible: The exact timing of moves is decided on the ground, by the herder, based on actual conditions. The guiding principle is that grasses need to recover from grazing. Each unit is grazed briefly, and recovers for the remainder of the summer. Additional resource goals—wildlife needs, riparian or other sensitive areas, endangered species issues—can be incorporated into the plan easily, because livestock grazing is so carefully controlled. And with a full-time herder, expensive fencing is not needed around every grazing unit. Natural features, electric fencing, mineral blocks, and well-trained dogs all contribute to controlling the herd's movements.

The West Elk Livestock Association's herding program has won awards from the Forest Service and from organizations of both range scientists and environmentalists. It has been so successful that the Forest Service granted a stocking rate *increase* a few years ago. While the challenges of herding are significant, so are the potential rewards, and the West Elks example proves that it can be done.

[For more information on herding and the West Elk Livestock Association, see the Quivira Coalition Newsletter of March 1999 (Vol. 2, No. 3).]

Intensity, p. 67.

Timing and Frequency.
The limitation of ADAs as a management tool is that they do not account for the other factors that determine the impacts of grazing: timing and frequency. If grazing occurs only in the dormant season, then ADAs can be an adequate tool by itself (see **Ghost Ranch: Grazing in the Dormant Season Only**, p. 73). But most ranches cannot destock for the growing season and restock again in the fall.

During the growing season, the challenge is to control the impact of grazing in such a way that the grasses have time to recover. David Ogilvie strives to have all his grasses set seed; Jim Winder's goal is to have all his grasses recover completely from grazing by the end of the growing season; put another way, his goal is zero percent utilization: no difference in biomass between grazed and ungrazed plants. (This may be unachievable, strictly speaking, but it's an important ideal to work towards.) Both David and Jim, like Sid Goodloe, Roger Bowe, and the Donaldsons, accomplish their goals by moving their cattle frequently. This way they can control the rest periods allowed for recovery.

It's impossible to know when it will rain, how much, or how long the growing season will last. So there's no telling exactly how

long it will take for grasses to recover from grazing. But the principles of growing season grazing management are fairly simple: 1) the more leaf area that's grazed off, the longer recovery will take, and 2) a plant that is grazed again before recovering will store less energy in its tissues and will weaken over time.

A rotational system mimics

[Top] A small plot on the Babbitt Ranch in Arizona with 840 head of cattle on it. [Bottom] Right after the cattle leave the plot. (Photos courtesy of Dan Dagget.)

The Babbitt Ranch plot in the next growing season after the animal impact pictured on p. 65. (Photo courtesy of Dan Dagget.)

the grazing patterns of wild ungulates in grassland environments. Each pasture is grazed for a short period of time, then allowed to rest. How precisely the timing and frequency of grazing can be controlled depends on the number of pastures in the rotation. Jim Winder and Roger Bowe calculate grazing periods this way:

Grazing period = Rest period divided by the number of pastures minus one

On the Bowe Ranch, with 62 pastures, two days of grazing are followed by 122 days of rest. When there were only 40 pastures and the rest period was only 78 days, the grasses weren't recovering, so either the grazing period had to be shorter or the number of pastures had to be increased. The same formula can be applied with smaller numbers of pastures as well. David Ogilvie, for

example, has sixteen pastures in the growing season rotation, so his grazing periods are longer, both absolutely and relative to rest periods. Because he rotates more slowly, however, his pastures rest for about a year before being grazed again.

In addition to rotation and rest, there is the issue of timing within the growing season. As pointed out earlier, grasses are more vulnerable to disturbance early in the growing season, when energy from the roots has been expended in producing leaves. Because different species of grass begin growing at different times, there is no single moment when grazing impacts are greatest. Moreover, cattle tend to select young, green plants. The practical point is thus that grazing should not happen at the same time of year every year in any given pasture. If it does, the palatable species that are young and green at that time will bear a disproportionate share of the impact and will eventually decline relative to other species. All of the ranchers profiled here change their rotations from year to year, so that the impact will be distributed more evenly across the plant species present.

66

Using ADAs to Control Grazing Intensity

To estimate ADAs, one begins with the amount of forage one animal consumes in one day. In weight, this is generally about 20-25 pounds of dry matter. Jim Winder initially measured ADAs by clipping and weighing sample plots to determine pounds of available forage per acre. Clipping only what a cow will easily eat, he then divides the results by 25 pounds to arrive at available ADAs. Over time he's developed an eye for what an ADA looks like, so clipping and weighing is no longer necessary.

Roger Bowe and others utilize a different technique. They begin by agreeing on a certain intensity of grazing they want to achieve: to graze the grass down to a short stubble, take half-leave half, leave three-quarters, etc. Then two people pace off an area, walking at a right angle to each other until they have walked two sides of a square (or rectangle) that looks like it contains enough forage to feed one animal for one day while leaving the desired amount of forage uneaten. Each pace is approximately one yard, so the area paced off is easily calculated in square yards. Since there are 4,840 square yards in an acre, the number of animal-days per acre is easily calculated from this simple estimate.

The advantages of managing intensity by using ADAs are practical ones. Theoretically, ADAs have some of the same shortcomings as carrying capacity and utilization rates. If the pasture is not uniform in productivity, then the square you pace off can be an inaccurate sample for the pasture as a whole. The scale problem thus remains. But ADAs are still more precise than other tools, because the units are small. And the pace method allows for continual improvement in your skill at estimating intensity. At the end of a grazing period, you can easily calculate the actual use of the pasture in ADAs, and then look at the ground: Are the plants half-eaten? Did the cattle graze it down to stubble? Any error in your estimate will be easily recognized by comparing actual use and intended intensity. Over time, ranchers using this method say they've become quite good at estimating ADAs accurately. Moreover, the pace method is fast and easy. It takes a couple of minutes and requires nothing more than a hand-held calculator. If conditions in a pasture are varied, it's easy to pace off a dozen different plots to try to improve your estimate.

Another advantage of ADAs is that the estimates can only be done after the grass has grown. The best time to calculate your available ADAs is at the end of the growing season. This means you are planning on the basis of what's already there, rather than on what might grow in the coming season. This reduces your exposure to an uncertain future. Jim Winder makes these calculations twice, at the end of the spring and the summer growing seasons.

In theory, the greater the intensity of grazing during the grazing period, the longer the rest period must be to allow for recovery. The ranches profiled here appear to confirm this: to increase intensity (i.e., stock more cattle on the same amount of land) requires a larger number of pastures. The ranches with higher stocking rates (Bowe and

"Perhaps the most controversial issue in livestock distribution concerns density. Should livestock graze together in a herd, or should they be spread out across the range?"

Winder) have many more pastures and much shorter grazing periods than those with lower stocking rates (Goodloe, Donaldson, and Ogilvie). The claim that rapid rotation allows for much higher stocking rates is disputed in the scientific literature, however. The safest conclusion seems to be that greater control over grazing in all its dimensions— timing, intensity, and frequency— may increase the productivity of the land, allowing for stocking rate increases over time.

Animal Distribution

Control over grazing boils down to control over the distribution of livestock across the range and over time. On the New Ranches we've examined, this is accomplished with fencing. It does not have to be five-strand, barbed-wire fence. Most interior fences are two-strand electric fence. Sid Goodloe uses three-strand, barbed-wire fences with the posts set 90 feet apart. Large staples hold the wire loosely against the posts, so that the wires can give a little when pressed by livestock.

There are other ways to control the distribution of livestock, of course. Mineral blocks have been used this way for decades. Where water can be turned on and off, it can also be used to control the location of grazing pressure. Herding is an ancient technique that is currently being reborn in a few areas. Riders and dogs are used to move and control the herd. There are also skilled practitioners of

stockmanship, who have mastered the art of "low-stress" livestock handling. These techniques require practice and education of animals and humans alike. Once perfected, stockmanship reduces stress on the livestock and makes it possible to move large numbers of animals with small inputs of time and labor. The effectiveness of these tools depends on the terrain and vegetation of a given range, the breeding and disposition of animals, and the inclinations and training of managers.

Perhaps the most controversial issue in livestock distribution concerns density. Should livestock graze together in a herd, or should they be spread out across the range? For decades, ranchers and range conservationists have worked to spread cattle out in order to utilize forage more evenly across large pastures. Clearly, it is desirable to avoid overutilizing certain areas while underutilizing others. The question is how to achieve this.

The New Ranchers have chosen to amalgamate their herds and work them as a single unit or, in certain circumstances, as two herds (to allow replacement heifers to acclimate without competition from older cows, for example). The benefits they attribute to this are several. A single herd is more easily monitored: Roger Bowe and Jim Winder both stress that they can see all their livestock quickly and easily, whenever they want. This decreases labor and other costs associated with routine care. Anyone who has spent a week or two gathering cattle spread

out over a large pasture knows that simply finding your animals can be very expensive. Cattle in a herd are also better able to fend off predators than if they were spread out, just as wild ungulates are. Given the importance of predators to environmentalists, this is a political advantage as well as an economic one.

Planning

The ranchers interviewed for this handbook are unanimous in saying that planning has been critical to their successes. Not only does good planning improve management, it also provides a greater sense of control over one's livelihood, an important boost to morale in a business characterized by uncertainty and risk. A lot of planning work is tedious: sitting at the computer, poring over monitoring results, keeping records. But as in any business, it pays off on the bottom line.

Plans should be flexible, but always ready for the worst. All of the ranchers profiled here, and several others I interviewed, stressed that they plan every year as if it will be a drought year. If the drought happens—as it does as often as not—they're ready for it. If it doesn't, they find themselves in a good position: to hold over some more calves, buy in some steers, or bank

the forage for the future.

Grazing Pressure. The central task of planning is to allocate grazing pressure. This includes when the grazing will occur, at what intensity, and for how long. Jim Winder divides this task into three components: inventory, allocation, and monitoring. By doing an inven-

An area on Roger Bowe's ranch before and after intense animal impact. The abundant plant in the top photo is broom snakeweed, an undesirable half-shrub. Cattle trampled it into the ground, and it was largely replaced by grasses. (Photos courtesy of Roger Bowe.)

> "Planning cannot be limited to a single year's grazing schedule. It must also anticipate the great variability of forage production over longer time periods."

tory, he learns how many ADAs are available on his ranch at the end of a growing season. He then allocates that forage, creating a sort of grazing budget. He knows exactly how long his present herd can feed in a given pasture and still leave enough leaf area for subsequent recovery. Jim also allocates a certain amount of biomass to wildlife needs and sets aside some forage for emergencies.

Together, inventory and allocation allow stocking decisions to be made well in advance, greatly reducing uncertainty. If he has 24,000 ADAs in a pasture, for example, then Jim knows he can graze 240 animals for 100 days. If 100 days won't be long enough to get him back to the growing season, he can destock now and be confident that the pasture will support 200 head for 120 days.

Finally, Jim monitors conditions in his pastures throughout the year. The amount of available forage in each pasture is recorded on a map of the ranch, using different colored pins to indicate degrees of use. Transects in each pasture are read after grazing and again at the end of the growing season to measure progress towards the goal of zero percent net primary production utilized.

Timing issues are easily incorporated into planning grazing pressure. The first question is which areas to graze in the dormant season and which in the growing season. Frequently, different areas will lend themselves to summer or winter use, due to elevation and climate. This

may mean staying out of rugged terrain in the hot summer months, when cattle will tend to congregate in low-lying, shaded areas and avoid the ridgetops. Or it may mean pushing the herd up into the mountains in the summer to cooler pastures, where snow may preclude winter grazing. Within the growing season, planning should consider grazing periods, rest periods, and any special circumstances associated with particular pastures, such as the presence of riparian areas or sensitive wildlife habitat. When Roger Bowe was first implementing his new system, he flagged individual grass plants and monitored their growth after grazing to determine how long his rest periods should be. Such questions can only be answered by careful evaluation of conditions specific to each ranch.

Managing for the Whole. Planning cannot be limited to a single year's grazing schedule. It must also anticipate the great variability of forage production over longer time periods. Jim Winder characterizes this as nature's "boom and bust" cycle. To plan for it requires attention to the ecological processes described in Chapter Three and awareness of thresholds of change, as discussed in Chapter Four. This means looking at more than just the forage, which is only one part of the system. What gets eaten by livestock is a function of numerous processes involving water, soils, decomposers, other plants, and so on.

The aim of planning in

"bust" periods (this usually means drought, but it can also be fires, insect infestations, diseases, or anything that reduces forage to very low levels) is to minimize the negative effects. In a short-duration grazing system, this may entail slowing the rotation, to allow longer rest periods for grasses to recover. In other systems, it may mean taking less forage off the range by decreasing grazing intensity. Often, this means destocking. Thresholds of negative change are easily crossed when plants are stressed, and long-term considerations may compel short-term austerity.

Droughts also stress troublesome species like snakeweed and burroweed, however, and may present management opportunities. If you must feed hay, for example, distribute it in an area infested with snakeweed and use the cattle's impact to set back the existing vegetation (see **Animal Impact**, p. 74).

Bust periods are worst on ranges that are already in poor condition, because the resilience of the system to disturbance has diminished. (For that matter, a degraded range can suffer in good times as well, when for instance a heavy rain event results in severe erosion.) Boom periods, on the other hand, represent opportunities to improve conditions and build the resilience of the range. Ideally, a boom will push an area across a threshold into a more desirable state: a more diverse community of vegetation, or a greater proportion of

perennial grasses, for example. In general, management should aim to increase ground cover (either live plants or litter) to protect the soil and to increase the diversity of vegetation. A more diverse range is better able to withstand disturbance.

Trigger Sites. Most ranches cannot afford to invest in expensive range restoration projects like chaining or seeding, except perhaps on small scales *[46]*. Funds are typically limited, and projects must be selected carefully to yield the greatest possible return on the dollar. The preceding chapters suggest some principles for making these decisions.

The greatest returns will result where natural processes of growth and recovery can be triggered or accelerated by management inputs. The range is not a uniform resource: certain areas have greater potential than others, due to the distribution of nutrients and water. These areas will yield the greatest amount of biomass per unit of management input, and should thus be the focus of restoration actions. They are *trigger sites*, naturally disposed to respond to management.

The best example, as mentioned earlier, is riparian areas. There are an increasing number of documented examples of riparian areas that have been restored simply by changing the timing of grazing to allow rest during the growing season. Phil Knight's Date Creek Ranch is perhaps the best known of these. Like Jim Winder's Macho Creek, Date Creek now provides more

"A more diverse range is better able to withstand disturbance."

forage than it did when it was grazed year-round. (See photos, p. 54.)

Trigger sites are not limited to riparian areas, however. David Ogilvie's burn program provides another example. Bear grass plants are trigger sites, at least when they are found beneath juniper trees, because they provide an input of energy (namely fuel) needed to kill the trees above them. Sid Goodloe creates trigger sites for his burns by pushing piñon-juniper trees up against each other with a bulldozer. The bulldozed trees dry out and become fuel for killing the adjacent, live trees. This allows Sid to kill more trees without having to pay the expense of bulldozing them.

Identifying trigger sites begins with an assessment of existing conditions. Where are water and nutrients unusually high? Is the ranch's natural system retaining and cycling them, or losing them? Second, some knowledge of the land's history is needed. What did the area used to look like? Were grasses more dominant? Were fires more common? Were there arroyos? By understanding what has changed, one gets a sense of what may be possible and what the obstacles to improvement are. Finally, how can management most economically intervene to shift the patterns of water and nutrient distribution toward the desired state? Answering this question may entail research or opportunistic experimentation. Sid Goodloe has discovered, for example, that cholla cactus can be removed with a cable without

resprouting, but only following a particular combination of dry and moist periods.

A good trigger site will lead to improvements beyond the area of direct management action. Increased grass cover on a hillslope, for example, may lead to greater water retention, which benefits areas downstream in the watershed. A functioning riparian channel will have a similar effect on the adjacent floodplain: more water will remain in the area, for a longer period of time, so that nearby plants can use it for growth.

Adaptive Management.
Planning is not complete until provision is made to monitor the effects of management actions and thereby learn from them. It should be clear from the preceding chapters that grazing is a much more complicated process than meets the eye, and that our knowledge of how it affects rangelands is far from complete. Careful, on-going monitoring complements the general principles discussed earlier and enables the manager to apply them, flexibly and creatively, on the ground. Without monitoring, mistakes may go unnoticed until it is too late to minimize the consequences, while successes may be misinterpreted. If Roger Bowe had not monitored for litter cover, his experiment might have resulted in tremendous damage to the ranch by overstocking. Then, he might have abandoned the whole thing (or lost the ranch), without learning that success was just around

"Planning is not complete until provision is made to monitor the effects of management actions and thereby learn from them."

Ghost Ranch: Grazing in the Dormant Season Only

On Ghost Ranch, near Abiquiu, New Mexico, Virgil Trujillo manages one of the West's most unusual and impressive grazing programs. The ranch consists of some 20,000 acres of deeded land in the grass-covered Chama River Basin, between 6,200 and 6,600 feet in elevation. It belongs to the Presbyterian Church, which runs the ranch as a retreat and guest resort. The unusual ownership situation has insulated the grazing program from the pressures of the beef market and allowed Virgil to manage things creatively.

Like most of the area's residents, Virgil can trace his family roots back centuries, to the early Hispanic period. For generations before the

Virgil Trujillo. (Photo courtesy of Courtney White.)

creation of the U.S. Forest Service, these Spanish-speaking families ran sheep and cattle through this country, using range resources in communal fashion. Today, the mountains surrounding Ghost Ranch are National Forest land, but communal arrangements are still the norm. Forest allotments are shared by many families, almost all of which have fewer than thirty head. Low cattle prices, competing demands on time, piñon-juniper encroachment, and shifting generational attitudes—all these things together imperil the community's traditional pastoralist lifeways.

Under Virgil's management, Ghost Ranch helps to buttress these traditions, while simultaneously stewarding the rangeland resources. The Forest allotments are buried in snow during the winter, and few families have sufficient lower-elevation rangelands to carry their animals. Ghost Ranch serves as a giant winter grazing ground for some fifty families, at reasonable rates and under a cooperative labor arrangement. The cattle are managed as a herd, under a rotational system which Virgil directs. The twenty-four pastures are each grazed for about two weeks between November and May. In the summer, the families move their cattle up into the mountains, and the Ghost Ranch lands rest. The long rest periods have allowed highly palatable species like winterfat (a classic "decreaser" in response to grazing) to thrive and increase, raising the carrying capacity of the ranch and, by extension, the durability of cultural traditions whose value cannot be translated into monetary terms.

the corner.

The New Ranch rests on the fact that rangelands can be managed in such a way that food is produced profitably and sustainably, with benefits for people, wildlife, soils, plants, and watersheds. The question is not whether this is possible but how to realize it. If it were easy, scientists would by now have figured

Animal Impact

Does vegetation benefit from being grazed by a concentrated herd rather than dispersed animals? Here the controversy is not yet resolved. Experiments have clearly shown that higher animal densities compact soil and thereby decrease rates of water infiltration in the short term, which by itself is bad for the water cycle *[29, 38, 87, 103, 104, 112, 113, 114, 115]*. Over the long term, indirect responses (such as increased root growth of plants) may overcome the effects of soil compaction, however. There is also some evidence that animals confined to smaller pastures for short periods of time graze plants more evenly, because they cannot be as selective *[83]*. This decreases the competitive imbalances associated with selective grazing and removes older, senescent materials from grasses *[3]*. (Other experiments have disputed this claim, however *[65]*.)

Animal impact is not as easy to study scientifically as one might think, because—like other disturbances—its effects depend on timing, intensity, and frequency. Under certain circumstances, it may resemble a fire: clearing out shrubs and tree seedlings and accelerating nutrient cycling, to the benefit of grasses (see below). If compounded by other disturbances, however, such as drought, it may remove cover and expose bare ground to erosion. There is not likely to be a single, conclusive judgment on animal impact. It may be good, bad, or indifferent, depending on a wide variety of factors in any given case. It is a tool which like all tools should be used judiciously.

The photos on p. 69 were taken by Roger Bowe to monitor the effects of a management intervention he made in an area of heavy broom snakeweed infestation. Using hay fed from the back of a truck, he attracted his herd to the area for one day. While feeding, the cattle stomped all over the snakeweed. Their hooves churned the soil, pushing the snakeweed and some of the hay into the top layer. Their manure deposited a high concentration of nutrients. The results are clear from the photos: almost no snakeweed and a lot of grass. High intensity disturbance pushed the area across some critical threshold. Maybe the outcome would have been different in a drought, or if a huge flood had occurred immediately after the treatment. For whatever set of reasons, however, the intervention worked. Those who have seen such things are convinced that animal impact can be a tool for range restoration.

it out much as they have for the production of other commodities like cars and steel and microchips. But it is not easy, because rangelands are complex natural systems characterized by great variability. No two ranches are the same, and in many ways every ranch is different every year. Each manager must be prepared to adapt based on particular conditions and circumstances—hence the term adaptive management—treating the challenge of sustainable ranching as a blend of artistry and experiment. Monitoring is the step that completes the loop of education, enabling the land to teach us how to manage it better.

The Williams Ranch
Quemado, New Mexico

"I think it's gonna work."
--*Jim Williams*

Jim Williams' mother and father bought the family ranch in 1931: nine and a half sections of private land along Largo Creek, south of the town of Quemado in Catron County. About ten years later, they acquired the permit to graze 22 sections of Forest Service land adjoining the home place. Jim has lived there all his life, and he still runs the ranch in partnership with his brother, Matt. The ranch lies above 7,000 feet of elevation and receives nine to twelve inches of precipitation in an average year.

In 1995, the Forest Service followed through on a threat it had made before: to cut the permit. In a review of its grazing permits, required under the National Environmental Policy Act (NEPA), Forest Service officials had concluded that Jim's allotment was in "poor to fair" condition. Blue grama,

the principal forage species, had increased to well over the twenty percent of vegetation called for in range condition descriptions; cool-season grasses were less than they should be. Henceforth, instead of year-round use, Jim would be permitted to graze the allotment only nine and a half months of the year, so that it could rest in the spring.

The cut impacted Jim's operation more than he expected. He had to keep all his cattle on his deeded lands through the spring, instead of only the cows that were calving. That increased the grazing pressure there and led to higher hay costs. "It crippled us," he says. The county appealed the NEPA findings for the whole Forest, but lost in court—something that never used to happen before.

In the summer of 1997, Jim volunteered to give a tour of his ranch to

Blue Grama

the Quivira Coalition, to look at the range and discuss what might be done. The range conservationist for the Forest Service attended, too. It was the first of many meetings to come. Previously, the higher half of the allotment was grazed each summer, and the lower half each winter. Jim and Quivira worked out a grazing plan for the whole ranch—summer, winter, and deeded areas—that ensures that every pasture rests for ninety days during the growing season. The Largo Creek riparian area is grazed during the winter dormant season, and for brief periods in the growing season. The plan required one well and a pipeline, to improve water distribution, but otherwise it changed nothing except the timing of grazing and recovery periods. Improvements in the riparian area were evident during the very next growing season. Good rains in the summer of 1999—the first year of the new system—produced dramatic improvements, especially in the riparian area. "It works," Jim says, even after serious drought in the summer of 2000.

Jim stresses three things about the change. First, he has learned a lot. The biggest change, for him, is all the people coming out to the ranch, for meetings and workshops and ranch tours. He and his wife don't have the privacy they used to, he admits, but it's worth it, because he always learns something. He'd never tried to calculate the forage available at the end of the growing season, for example, or to plan his grazing accordingly. "We just moved the cows around and used the forage however." It makes sense that Largo Creek would improve most quickly, he realizes now, but it hadn't occurred to him before.

Second, better monitoring has improved Jim's control over both his grazing and his future. Before, the only

data were collected by the Forest Service, using the Parker 3-step method and the old range condition model. The blue grama, combined with encroachment by piñon and juniper trees, resulted in low condition scores. Using a newer model, however, scientists from the Jornada Experimental Range concluded that, in terms of rangeland health, Jim's allotment was fully functional: Many areas could not be expected to support cool season grasses, and the soil stability and watershed function of the allotment were good. In addition to range monitoring with help from the Jornada, Jim is also monitoring his riparian area, in cooperation with a retired Forest Service biologist. Getting your own data is really important, he says. It gives him a "second opinion," so to speak, to confirm or challenge the judgments of the Forest Service. And down the road, if he ever ends up in court, he'll have data to support his management.

Finally, relations with the Forest Service have improved substantially. "In 1995, we were barely talking," Jim says. Now they're working together, on the allotment and on Jim's private lands. They're listening, experimenting, and learning. The additional monitoring data are welcome, since the Forest Service doesn't have the staff and resources to do as much as it would like. More information makes everyone more confident in the decisions they make, and more comfortable trying new ideas, because they know the results will be documented and reviewed. On-the-ground improvements mean a lot, especially in the riparian areas. And now, Jim and the Forest Service have more to discuss than just stocking rates. He's hopeful the 1995 cuts will be restored some day. "I think it's gonna work," he says.

Chapter Six
Making the Leap

"The answers, if they are to come and if they are to work, must be developed in the presence of the user and the land; they must be developed to some degree *by* the user *on* the land."

--Wendell Berry

Making Changes on the Ground

The principles of the New Ranch are based on the biology of plants and livestock and the ecology of rangelands. Scientists are constantly working to learn more about these topics, and it can seem impossible to keep up with the literature. But for a ranch manager, knowing all the details and debates is not likely to be that important. A basic familiarity with the principles will do.

After all, the real challenge is one that the scientists rarely have to confront: How to make a sustainable living from a piece of rangeland. Applying the knowledge is far more difficult than gathering it. Ranchers who've been around long

enough have probably seen all sorts of "new" ideas for range management come and go. Many have grown skeptical, if not downright resistant, to suggestions from outsiders. When presented with a new proposal for management, they offer a list of reasons why it "won't work on my country" or with "my cows."

Change is not easy. It falls in the domain of human habits and attitudes rather than scientific knowledge. "The way we've always done it" is a powerful guide for many ranchers. But the fact is that ranching in much of the West is squeezed from all sides: agencies imposing new restrictions in reaction to political pressure or lawsuits, development raising the prices of land, weather

Selective thinning on the Carrizo Valley Ranch. (Photo courtesy of Sid Goodloe.)

himself insists that the key to holistic management is *how you make decisions* rather than any particular grazing system. Most of the New Ranchers profiled in earlier chapters agree with this judgment. It may be that how they approached change— as much as the changes themselves— enabled them to succeed, and this might explain why their experiences seem at odds with the results of scientific experiments (see **The Debate Over Short-Duration Grazing**, p 22).

Examine your Goals

that remains unpredictable, and economic trends that have steadily eroded profitability. Times have changed, and ranching will have to change too. It may feel like a leap, but leaping is still preferable to being shoved over the edge by forces beyond your control.

Many of the ranchers profiled here report that *deciding* to change their management was the hardest part. The changes themselves grew easier with time, because ecological and economic goals aligned and reinforced each other. *An ecologically healthy ranch is a more profitable ranch.* The New Ranch benefits wildlife, watersheds, and biological diversity, *and* it benefits ranchers.

This final chapter offers some suggestions for making the leap, based on the experience of ranchers and ranching experts who've been through it before. Many of the suggestions echo those made by Allan Savory *[93]*. Savory

Ask yourself: What are your goals for the ranch? How does the ranch contribute to realizing goals for yourself, your family, your employees, your community? These may seem like silly or abstract questions, but they are fundamentally important, and answering them will help to clarify what to do. If your Number One goal is to make more money, then the changes you make should reflect that priority. Very likely, you also value the way of life that the ranch supports: working outdoors, with family, caring for your stock, being on the land. Perhaps keeping the ranch intact, in the family, is your highest goal, and making money is simply a means to that end. Examine these questions with the other people who have an interest in the ranch— family, employees, perhaps neighbors—and try to come to an understanding of how your goals relate to each other. Think of it as writing a mission statement for your ranch. It will probably include specific goals

for the land, for yourself and other people, and for economic performance.

Take Stock of your Operation

After you've examined your goals, do a careful assessment of your present operation. In broad terms, this should include the people, the land, and the financial resources that keep the ranch going, as well as the details of your management.

People. In any business, organization is extremely important. A great deal depends on how people relate to each other and to their responsibilities. What are the "human resources" available to your operation? What are each person's strengths, weaknesses, goals, and priorities? Are decisions getting made well and communicated effectively? Are responsibilities clearly defined? Effective cooperation is critical, and people work best when their morale is high. Even if your ranch seems like a small organization, involving only your family or a handful of employees, improving the way you work can save money and hassles. If you lease federal or state lands for grazing, you may spend a lot of time and energy embroiled in disputes with bureaucrats. How much does this effort benefit you or your ranch? Might there be other, more effective ways to approach these problems?

Land. How well do you know your land? Its history? How do its various components—soils, plants, water, insects, wildlife, sunlight—fit together? The research surveyed in preceding chapters suggests that little things like litter cover and termites may be critically important to producing forage, especially in dry years. What condition are they in on your range? How effective is rainfall? How common is drought? When is the natural forage at its highest quality for livestock nutrition?

The goals you set for the land must reflect both existing conditions and the potential for change (upwards and downwards). You may need to consult with range scientists, or track down old photographs or accounts, to learn what plants could grow where on your ranch, whether an arroyo was once a flowing creek, or whether trees like mesquite or juniper have encroached on grasses over time. In the course of this research, you can begin to identify trigger sites, and to evaluate priorities for change. Then you can evaluate your improvements: Are there areas you can't use in dry years because of unreliable water? How effectively can you control the timing of grazing on each pasture, using fences, water supplies, natural features, or other tools?

Financial Resources. Economic sustainability requires that your ranch operate in the black, generating returns adequate to cover costs and for reinvestment in the operation. Examine the financial make-up of your ranch: How much capital is tied up in land, equipment, improvements, and so on? Are those

"The goals you set for the land must reflect both existing conditions and the potential for change (upwards and downwards)."

Jim Williams' riparian area on Largo Creek, during dormant season grazing (above) and the next summer (below). (Photos courtesy of Courtney White.)

calving in mid-winter on Jim Winder's ranch). Finally, how much reserve capital is available? What other demands may be placed on those reserves—to pay for college expenses, for example? What are the long-term financial issues facing the ranch, such as estate taxes?

Return-on-investment in ranching is notoriously low, especially in areas where real estate speculation has driven up land values. Achieving a better return may require reducing costs of production, diversifying your operation, improving marketing, or capturing equity through sale of development rights or conservation easements [1, 88, 99]. (If your ranch is profitable, you also may be able to donate easements and significantly reduce your income tax burden.) A variety of government and non-profit organizations offer grants to do things that might benefit your operation: restoring a wetland, for instance, will benefit water quality and waterfowl habitat, while providing an important forage reserve for dry times.

assets producing sufficient returns to justify the investment? It may turn out that management practices that made sense in the past don't pay for themselves any more and should be discontinued (putting up hay on the McNeil Ranch, for example, or

Principles for Planning

According to the ranchers profiled here, planning is the

Managing to Cope with Predators

The issue of predators—wolves, mountain lions, coyotes, bears, bobcats—has divided the ranching and environmentalist communities for at least thirty years. Environmentalists are appalled by the record of government predator control programs, especially in regards to wolves and grizzly bears, which were exterminated from the majority of their ranges in the West. This work, performed by Animal Damage Control (now Wildlife Services), was justified politically by the need to protect sheep and cattle. Today, ironically, other government agencies are spending millions of dollars to reintroduce wolves and protect grizzlies. Coyotes and mountain lions have eluded elimination for a number of reasons, and there is some evidence that broad-scale coyote control programs are futile or even counter-productive.

Clearly, predators can kill livestock, and some individuals do make sheep or cattle into a regular part of their diets. Environmentalists are correct, however, that predators play important roles in ecosystems. Most feed on wild prey—elk, deer, or rabbits, for example—exerting control on their populations to the benefit of vegetation. These days, with elk numbers exploding in parts of the Southwest, more wolves could actually benefit grazing interests. It is also true that livestock can be managed in ways that minimize the threat of predator damage: stock can be kept in a herd, to maximize their natural defenses; calving can be timed or located to minimize exposure to hungry predators; as Sid Goodloe does, a few cattle of more aggressive breeds can be kept to help ward off predators.

Jim Winder's experience is telling. In the past fourteen years, Jim has had to kill only two coyotes to protect his stock. When Animal Damage Control advised him that there were lots of coyotes on his ranch, and suggested a program of control, Jim told them not to bother. During calving season, Jim sees coyotes consuming afterbirth, but they do not attempt to take on the herd of mother cows protecting their young. Jim sees a marketing opportunity, too: He can sell his beef at a premium because it's "predator-friendly."

When a predator habitually kills livestock, most environmentalists would agree that a problem exists, if only because livestock are not part of the predator's natural diet. The animal can best be removed or killed in a humane manner by people skilled in tracking and hunting. But wholesale, prophylactic predator control is difficult to justify in this day and age. By modifying livestock management, the predator issue can be resolved on the ground, where it counts.

single most important part of managing the New Ranch. Here again, the need is common to any business, except that ranching depends heavily on the unpredictable forces of nature. A few principles for planning follow.

Work with Natural Processes, Not Against Them. Our knowledge of how the range functions is not great enough to enable us to control it. Decades of attempts to manipulate range vegetation have failed or proved uneconomical *[89]*. The key is to work with the natural processes that drive forage production and range restoration. Examples from the ranches profiled here include:

● Timing breeding to occur when natural forage conditions are at their peak. This raises pregnancy rates without incurring high supplement costs. Similarly, by weaning calves just before the first frost, cows are better able to maintain condition when natural forage quality declines.

● Excluding livestock from riparian areas during the growing season. These areas will produce more forage than any other part of the range, if they're allowed to grow to their potential. Dormant season grazing of riparian areas is a simple, economical way to improve overall productivity. If your cattle depend on the water, the cost of installing a trough nearby will more than pay for itself in increased forage.

● Controlling grazing to allow grasses the time they need for recovery. This can be done in a number of ways—rotations, herding, controlling water sources, various kinds of fencing, etc. Recovery from disturbance is a natural process that cannot be controlled—but it can be accommodated.

● Finding management solutions to cope with predators (see **Managing to Cope with Predators**, p. 81).

● Using livestock as a tool to trigger ecological processes of recovery. Where overrest has occurred, for example, cattle can help remove decadent plant material, expose growth points to sunlight, break up soil capping, and increase grass cover.

● Using fire as a tool to control shrubs and trees. Fire is a complex topic and requires extensive cooperation with agencies and neighbors; it may not be an appropriate tool in some areas. But it is an important natural process in much of the West, and far more economical than other treatment options.

● Varying your rotation from year to year, so that your cattle do not select the same plant species in each pasture every year.

Figure 8. Annual Variation in Precipitation and Grass Yield, 1960-1988 [51].

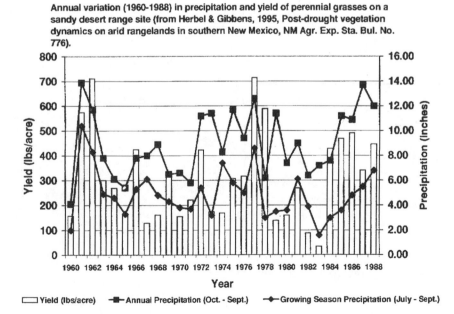

Annual variation (1960-1988) in precipitation and yield of perennial grasses on a sandy desert range site (from Herbel & Gibbens, 1995, Post-drought vegetation dynamics on arid rangelands in southern New Mexico, NM Agr. Exp. Sta. Bul. No. 776).

● Accelerating your rotation in wet years, and slowing it down in dry years, to match recovery periods to growth rates.

● Setting stocking rates according to existing available forage, instead of relying on fixed carrying capacity estimates or betting on the rains. There is no one "correct" stocking rate for range-lands where forage production can vary so much from one year to the next. Instead of trying to force the range to carry the same numbers every year, change the size of the herd to accommodate changing range conditions [82].

Drought isn't the Exception, It's the Rule. In arid and semiarid regions, drought is a common occurrence. Over a 29-year period at the Jornada Experimental Range, fourteen years were sufficiently dry that the range produced about half of the average forage yield (see Figure 8) [51]. In rough terms, forage was *half of normal half of the time*. During a drought, grazing is much more likely to cause damage to the range, because plants recover much more slowly. Poor management during a drought can hurt your range for years to come. For all these reasons, it pays to plan as though every year will be dry.

The following principles for drought management are taken from Kirk Gadzia's article in the *August 2000 Quivira Coalition newsletter (Vol. 3, No. 4)*:

● Do your dormant season planning! Assume no more forage

Seriously degraded rangeland on the San Carlos Apache Reservation in Arizona. (Photo courtesy of Phil Ogden.)

will grow. Determine how much existing forage there is and how long it will last with current numbers or various stock reduction options.

● Become accurate at estimating Animal Days per Acre (ADAs) of forage on the land in various conditions.

● Combine herds as soon as possible. Combining herds gives you more flexibility and reduces grazing periods relative to recovery periods.

● Increase recovery periods for pastures as much as possible.

● Be creative about increasing pasture numbers per herd. Use temporary fencing and work with others to combine herds and increase the number of pastures available.

● Plan long-term water availability and volume. Put your plan into action when times are good.

● Remember that drought effects are less severe when the water cycle is functioning effectively. Plan your grazing carefully at all times.

● Be prepared to vary stock numbers according to a stock reduction plan.

● Reduce numbers early, according to predetermined critical dates. Prices will be better and there will be more feed for the remaining stock.

● For breeding herds, wean offspring early. Consider options such as delayed breeding and/or reduced breeding vs. selling your genetics.

● Remember that drought feeding is rarely a good investment. Calculate the costs and make the comparisons yourself.

● Ensure your enterprise mix is compatible with drought risk in your area.

By applying these principles, Jim Winder runs more cattle during droughts now than he did normally under his old management. He has invested in wells, storage tanks, and waterlines to ensure that he can provide water anywhere on his ranch even in a bad drought. He calculates his stocking rate based on existing forage, measured at the end of the growing season every year (October) and monitored as the year progresses. This way, he knows exactly how many cattle he can support, for how long, even if it doesn't rain at all. He destocks early in dry times, when prices are better, so that he doesn't have to cut the herd more drastically later on. He runs a combined herd of stockers and cows, so he can destock (by selling the stockers) without selling his breeding animals *[82]*. These measures have resulted in improved range conditions, which means droughts don't affect his forage as much as they used to, and recovery from drought is more rapid.

The Hard Work is the Office Work. Planning is not easy work, and it's not often fun, either. It's not very exciting to keep careful records of actual use, rainfall, available forage, vegetation, etc. But it's extremely important. Your decisions can only be as good as the information they're based on, and gathering and evaluating information requires hours in the office or at the computer. Jim Winder emphasizes the distinction between "five dollar an hour jobs and hundred dollar an hour jobs." Fixing a fence is a five dollar an hour job, and you shouldn't let it get in the way of doing the hundred dollar an hour jobs—like planning the grazing rotation or monitoring its results. Time is money, and you should manage it carefully, because labor is too expensive to misallocate.

Manage for the Whole, Not Just a Few Parts. It's tempting to think that there's one thing that matters more than anything else: stocking rates, or weight gain, or pregnancy rates, or litter cover, or whathaveyou. But the range isn't so easily reduced to a single factor. Look for the relationships that sustain the range: how rain interacts with soils and plants, how grazing affects plant growth and litter cover, how the timing of moisture affects what plants grow.

Expect to Make Mistakes. Plans always include assumptions

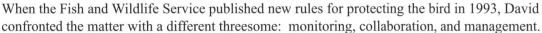
Endangered Species

What should you do if an endangered species is found on your ranch? "Shoot, shovel, and shut up," ran the old maxim. New Ranchers like David Ogilvie are working to find a new and better approach. The U Bar Ranch, which David manages, is home to the largest and most successful population of endangered Southwestern Willow Flycatchers anywhere. When the Fish and Wildlife Service published new rules for protecting the bird in 1993, David confronted the matter with a different threesome: monitoring, collaboration, and management.

Monitoring was necessary because very little was known about the remaining Willow Flycatchers. Livestock grazing and agriculture were presumed—by environmentalists and the Fish and Wildlife Service—to hurt the birds, but there wasn't strong evidence one way or the other. This is not unusual: These days, most species that become listed are listed *because very little is known about them.* Without scientific information, the Fish and Wildlife Service cannot defend inaction in the face of lawsuits. Research really only begins *after* a listing occurs.

On the U Bar, basic monitoring of the Willow Flycatchers began in 1994. Over the following four years, the population increased from 64 breeding pairs to 186. Since the monitoring protocol was the official one, established by the Fish and Wildlife Service, the agency could not dispute that the habitat on the U Bar was, if anything, improving.

Of course, critics might still complain that the ranch's monitoring data were suspect. Hence the need for collaboration with authoritative outside scientists. In 1997, the U Bar invited three scientists (one from Rocky Mountain Research Station and two from Western New Mexico University) to conduct more detailed research on the ranch's Willow Flycatcher populations. The results challenged several common notions about the bird's habitat needs, while further documenting the fact that grazing and farming were not threatening the endangered species. On the contrary, they may actually be beneficial.

David is an avid hunter and outdoorsman, and his management philosophy readily embraces wildlife needs. With credible data and research in hand, he not only can defend his management of the U Bar, but he can actively manage for the Willow Flycatcher: by curtailing farming work during the nesting season, for example, and by stabilizing the river banks to help maintain habitat (and, at the same time, protect his fields from erosion). He can continue to graze the area in a controlled and monitored fashion, steadily accumulating data that shows that cows and Flycatchers are compatible.

We can expect that more stories like David's will emerge in the years to come. After all, if an endangered species occupies a ranch, where grazing is managed better today than in decades past, chances are that the species is either unaffected by grazing or, quite possibly, benefits from it. With monitoring, collaboration, and management, there's no reason to fear the next endangered species.

[For more on the U Bar Ranch and the Southwestern Willow Flycatcher, see the September 1998 issue of the Quivira Coalition Newsletter (vol. 2, no. 1).]

about how things will happen, and these assumptions may prove incorrect. Mistakes should be expected, and viewed as opportunities to learn and improve the plan. Be sure to build into your plan the time and means to evaluate it and alter it, if necessary, before the consequences are too great. Monitoring plays an essential role in this process.

"Monitoring plays an essential role..."

Collaborate and Communicate

Managing rangelands well is not easy, especially given today's complex array of conservation issues: watersheds, open space, recreation, grazing, endangered species, etc. It's impossible to keep up with all the issues and information on your own. Too often, issues remain unaddressed until a crisis erupts: a lawsuit, an endangered species, a severe drought. New regulations are suddenly announced, new restrictions imposed, and another round of accusations ensues. In a swamp of distrust and bad feeling, even small steps forward become difficult.

Collaboration can be an effective way to bring together the expertise needed to identify problems and craft solutions before a crisis paralyzes everyone *[23]*. Often, the real problem is inadequate information, and the solution is simply better monitoring (see **Endangered Species**, p. 85). More generally, a lack of communication isolates people and keeps them from recognizing common interests and goals. Seeking the input of neigh-

bors, scientists, environmentalists, or agency personnel puts the ball in their court, so to speak, to describe their goals and suggest ways to achieve them. It also builds trust and confidence: Instead of an endless stalemate, there's a willingness to experiment, monitor, and gradually move toward resource goals. On the Empire Ranch, the Biological Planning Team has worked through a thicket of contentious issues. People from all sides of the grazing debate have learned from each other and helped improve conditions for cattle and wildlife alike. Similar exchanges have occurred through the Diablo Trust of Flagstaff, Arizona; the Malpai Borderlands Group in southeastern Arizona and southwestern New Mexico; the Valle Grande Grass Bank in northern New Mexico; the West Elks Livestock Association in southwestern Colorado; and on Deep Springs Ranch in eastern California.

Perceptions have often been more important than facts in fueling the grazing debate and preventing solutions. A defensive posture reaffirms critics in their conviction that ranchers don't value the environment and are trying to hide something. Openness and communication undercuts these prejudices. The extreme critics may refuse to engage in any constructive dialogue, but many more people will welcome the chance to learn and to contribute, as Jim Williams has discovered to his benefit. Everyone gains from improved management, and good management has nothing to hide.

CONCLUSION
Find and Expand the Radical Center

"...it is hard to be pessimistic about the West. This is the native home of hope. When it fully learns that cooperation, not rugged individualism, is the pattern that most characterizes and preserves it, ...it has a chance to create a society to match its scenery."

--*Wallace Stegner*

The six ranches profiled in the preceding chapters are by no means an exhaustive sample of New Ranch management, but they are sufficient to demonstrate that the New Ranch is not some far-off future fantasy. It already exists. Grazing can be managed in ways that are economically and ecologically sustainable, even in areas that receive less than twelve inches of rainfall per year. The aim of this short book has been to answer two questions. First, what do these innovative managers do? And second, why do their practices work?

The ranch profiles aimed to answer the first question, if only in brief. Sid Goodloe, David Ogilvie, John and Mac Donaldson, Roger Bowe, Jim Winder, and Jim Williams all admit that they do not know everything about the lands they manage—no one does. They emphasize the need to continue learning and changing their management to meet the particular (and dynamic) circumstances they face. In landscapes as complex and variable as these, management must be alert to a wide array of factors and flexible enough to adjust quickly.

The results that these ranchers have achieved are facts, and they must eventually be explainable in the light of scientific knowledge. To answer the second question, then, each chapter examined the challenge of sustainable ranching in terms of

Mine reclamation project in Globe, Arizona, using cattle. (Photo courtesy of Dan Dagget.)

of vegetation. Livestock exclusion (the tool of rest) will not necessarily result in a "natural" return to prior or "climax" conditions.

● Critical thresholds of change are generally crossed when two or more disturbances overlap or coincide (drought and heavy grazing, for example). Because many disturbances are unpredictable and beyond human control, the management of grazing must involve careful planning, monitoring, and a high degree of flexibility. To promote improvement across thresholds, management must also be opportunistic.

ecological processes: the growth of grasses, the grazing of plants by herbivores, and the cycling of water and nutrients over space and time. The key points that emerged are these:

● Grazing is a type of disturbance. Like other disturbances, its effects may be understood in terms of timing, intensity and frequency. Unlike many disturbances, grazing can be managed in terms of these same variables.

● Natural ecosystems are adapted to tolerate disturbance, within limits. Exactly what these limits are varies from place to place, depending on the natural history of the system in question. With a few exceptions, science has yet to define these limits in quantitative detail.

● In arid and semiarid rangeland ecosystems, the Clementsian model of succession must be modified to account for critical thresholds of change and multiple stable states

● Conclusions reached at one scale of experimentation or observation cannot always be extrapolated to other scales, because the processes driving rangeland ecosystems are scale-dependent. This is the case along both spatial and temporal dimensions. Conventional tools of range management have generally not recognized the degree to which the problem of scale limits their effectiveness in practice.

● Management tools that are crafted in terms of ecological processes are better suited to handle the problem of scale. The more carefully grazing can be managed in terms of timing, intensity, and frequency, the more likely it is to be sustainable.

● The ecological processes relevant to grazing come together at the surface of the ground, where plants (living, dormant, and dead) interact with soils, water, sunlight, decomposers, and disturbances. "Bare ground," as Roger Bowe puts it, "is the rancher's number one enemy."

Perhaps, in time, scientists will craft experiments that will prove or disprove these points. For the present, all people with an interest in rangelands must grapple with a substantial degree of uncertainty: We simply do not have any single prescription for "the best" management of these lands. Even with the best science, range management remains a craft: a blend of knowledge, experience, experimentation, artistry, and skill. Given the tremendous diversity of Western rangelands, flexible strategies of management and research, tailored to local needs and circumstances, seem most likely to yield significant advances.

For a time, the goal of range management seemed fairly clear: produce more food. This was understood to benefit both ranchers and the public at large. Expensive manipulations of rangeland were evaluated against fairly simple cost-benefit ratios. Nowadays the goals and expectations aren't nearly so simple. In many peoples' judgment, food is a low priority for public rangelands; biodiversity, water quality, wildlife habitat, recreation, and open space might all rank higher in a poll of mainstream American opinion. With the partial exception of recreation, however, none of these values yet lend themselves to sustaining rural economies and communities. And without rural communities, a significant piece of the conservation puzzle will be lost.

Of course, the economics of range livestock production are not particularly favorable to the long-term viability of ranching. There is a growing body of information on ways that ranchers can improve their financial prospects by capitalizing on values other than livestock: conservation easements, purchase of development rights, ecotourism, niche marketing, diversification [1, 88, 99]. These are valuable and important new ideas, and more can be expected in years to come. But none of these things, alone or in combination, can supplant good land management—stewardship—as the overarching priority, because the other values all come down, sooner or later, to conserving and enhancing healthy landscapes. The potential of rangelands to produce values to society—however they may be defined—inevitably depends on the stability of the soil, the integrity of water, nutrient, and energy cycles, and the ability of the ecosystem to recover from disturbance [78]. Producing food is not the only valuable use of rangelands—far from it—but it depends on the same ecological processes as all the others.

Today, some environmental extremists insist that the arid western range must be free of cattle [28]. Some in the ranching community react by insisting that there's no problem out there at all. Both extremes are wrong. In many areas—especially arid ones—excluding cattle

"In many areas—especially arid ones—excluding cattle would do almost nothing to improve ecological conditions. Thresholds have long since been crossed, and natural succession will not restore 'pristine' nature..."

Subdivision in Wyoming. (Photo courtesy of Dan Dagget.)

would do almost nothing to improve ecological conditions. Thresholds have long since been crossed, and natural succession will not restore "pristine" nature [85]. On the other hand, there are genuine resource issues out there on the range: the enduring effects of historic over-grazing, the growing impacts of recreation and subdivision, and a widening array of social demands on range resources for open space, water, wildlife, and so on. Throwing the ranchers off and walking away is not an answer, but neither is denying the problems that do exist.

In the center, between these extremes, lies a truly radical solu-tion, in the sense that it gets to the root of the issue: the actual condi-tions of the range and what can really be done about them. This solution depends on people who share an enduring commitment to particular landscapes working together to craft programs that achieve genuine conservation using available tools: science, fire, rest,

grazing, animal impact, innovative minds, and common sense. These are grassroots programs, both literally and metaphorically.

The radical center is grow-ing, and it represents an important resource for ranchers seeking to meet today's challenges. The experience of the Quivira Coalition and the ranchers profiled here is that many people are interested in participating, and most are not closed-minded or righteous. The public is full of folks who seek more contact with the land and the people who live on it. Many have valuable skills to contribute. The public is also, effectively, both judge and jury in deciding the fate of public lands ranching over the long haul.

Collaboration and communi-cation are the essence of the radical center. Collaboration brings people together; communication allows them to learn from one another and spread the word to others. One might expect the public lands agencies to take the lead in these activities, but they are generally too understaffed, too paralyzed by litigation, too politi-cized, and/or too bureaucratic to do so. Leadership will have to come from outside.

Examples of the radical center are popping up across the West. Ranchers, agency personnel, scientists and environmentalists are coming together and discovering that they have common visions for the lands they share, and that they actually enjoy working out creative ways to realize those visions. The issues that spark the meetings are various: endangered species issues, the threat of subdivision, the need to restore fire to control shrubs or trees. The process is rarely fast or trouble-free. But it's more promising than the alternatives: more lawsuits, continued agency paralysis, ongoing conversion to ranchettes, rural economic decline, and environmental issues left unaddressed.

As the methods and philosophy of the New Ranch spread, it may be hoped that the acrimonious and litigious and often counter-productive "rangeland conflict" will run out of fuel and finally expire. Yes, rangelands have suffered, tremendously, from overgrazing in the past; yes, the damage persists to this day in many areas. But the damage is done, and there is no benefit in persecuting the living for the actions of the dead. It is not *cattle*, but management, that determines the impacts of grazing. And management today is nothing like it was a century ago. The greatest threat to Western landscapes today is not livestock grazing but urbanization *[35, 47]*, a land use that feeds on the economic decline of ranching.

Real, on-the-ground solutions will not come from national legislation or precedent-setting litigation, because range livestock production depends on natural ecosystems and natural ecosystems are everywhere different. Steward-ship is as much a social process as an ecological one, and it does not often happen from the top down. The best hope for the land lies in local people who care enough to

work and learn together on and from the ground that unites them. It is time for reasonable people—ranchers, environmentalists, agency personnel, and scientists—to desist from the hatred and hyperbole of the past thirty years and get to work.

Upland improvement on the Double Lightning Ranch. [Top] 1986. [Bottom] 1994. (Photos courtesy of Jim Winder.)

Bibliography

> "All great truths
> begin as
> blasphemies."
> --George Bernard
> Shaw

1. Anderson, B. 2000. *The New Frontiers of Ranching: Business Diversification and Land Stewardship.* Tucson: Sonoran Institute.

2. Anderson, D.M. 1982. Seasonal grazing of semidesert tobosa rangeland in southern New Mexico. *In* D.D. Briske and M.M. Kothmann, eds. *Proceedings: A National Conference on Grazing Management Technology,* pp. 137-142. Texas A&M University, November 10-12.

3. Anderson, D.M. 1988. Seasonal stocking of tobosa managed under continuous and rotation grazing. *Journal of Range Management* 41(1): 78-83.

4. Archer, S. 1989. Have southern Texas savannas been converted to woodlands in recent history? *American Naturalist* 134(4): 545-561.

5. Archer, S. 1994. Woody plant encroachment into Southwestern grasslands and savannas: Rates, patterns and proximate causes. *In* Martin Vavra, William A. Laycock and Rex D. Pieper, eds. *Ecological Implications of Livestock Herbivory in the West,* pp. 13-68. Denver: Society for Range Management.

6. Archer, S. and F.E. Smeins. 1991. Ecosystem-level processes. *In* R.K. Heitschmidt and J.W. Stuth, eds. *Grazing Management: An Ecological Perspective,* pp. 109-139. Portland, Oregon: Timber Press.

7. Bahre, C.J. 1991. *A Legacy of Change: Historic Human Impact on*

Bibliography

the Vegetation of the Arizona Borderlands. Tucson: University of Arizona Press.

8. Belnap, J. and D.A. Gilbert. 1998. Vulnerability of desert biological soil crusts to wind erosion: The influences of crust development, soil texture, and disturbance. *Journal of Arid Environments* 39: 133-142.

9. Belsky, A.J. 1986. Does herbivory benefit plants? A review of the evidence. *American Naturalist* 127(6): 870-892.

10. Belsky, A.J. 1992. Effects of grazing, competition, disturbance and fire on species composition and diversity in grassland communities. *Journal of Vegetation Science* 3: 187-200.

11. Belsky, A.J., W.P. Carson, C.L. Jensen, and G.A. Fox. 1993. Overcompensation by plants: Herbivore optimization or red herring? *Evolutionary Ecology* 7: 109-121.

12. Bentley, H.L. 1898. Cattle Ranges of the Southwest: A History of the Exhaustion of the Pasturage and Suggestions for its Restoration. U.S. Department of Agriculture Farmer's Bulletin No. 72. Washington, D.C.: Government Printing Office.

13. Beymer, R.J. and J.M. Klopatek. 1992. Effects of grazing on cryptogamic crusts in pinyon-juniper woodlands in Grand Canyon National Park. *American Midland Naturalist* 127(1): 139-148.

14. Bork, E.W. and S.J. Werner. 1999. Viewpoint: Implications of spatial variability for estimating forage use. *Journal of Range Management* 52(2): 151-156.

15. Briggs, M.K. 1996. *Riparian Ecosystem Recovery in Arid Lands: Strategies and References.* Tucson: University of Arizona Press.

16. Briske, D.D. 1991. Developmental morphology and physiology of grasses. *In* Rodney K. Heitschmidt and Jerry W. Stuth, eds. *Grazing Management: An Ecological Perspective,* pp. 85-108. Portland, Oregon: Timber Press.

17. Briske, D.D. 1999. Plant traits determining grazing resistance: Why have they proved so elusive? *In* D. Eldridge and D. Freudenberger, eds. *People and Rangelands: Building the Future,* pp. 899-905. Proceedings of the VI International Rangeland Congress.

18. Briske, D.D. and R.K. Heitschmidt. 1991. An ecological perspective. *In* R.K. Heitschmidt and J.W. Stuth, eds. *Grazing Management: An Ecological Perspective,* pp. 11-26. Portland, Oregon: Timber Press.

19. Briske, D.D. and J.H. Richards. 1994. Physiological responses of individual plants to grazing: Current status and ecological significance. *In* M. Vavra, W.A. Laycock and R.D. Pieper, eds. *Ecological Implications of Livestock Herbivory in the West,* pp. 147-176. Denver: Society for Range Management.

20. Brown, B.J. and T.F.H. Allen. 1989. The importance of scale in evaluating herbivory. *Oikos* 54: 189-194.

21. Brown, J.R., J.E. Herrick and D. Price. 1999. Managing low-output agroecosystems sustainably: The importance of ecological thresholds. *Canadian Journal of Forest Research* 29: 1112-1119.

22. Brummer, J.E., R.L. Gillen and F.T. McCollum, 1988. Herbage dynamics of tallgrass prairie under short duration grazing. *Journal of Range Management* 41(3): 264-266.

23. Cestero, B. 1999. *Beyond the Hundredth Meeting: A Field Guide to Collaborative Conservation on the West's Public Lands.* Tucson: Sonoran Institute.

24. Collins, S.L. 1987. Interaction of disturbances in tallgrass prairie: A field experiment. *Ecology* 68(5): 1243-1250.

25. Collins, S.L. and S.C. Barber. 1985. Effects of disturbance on diversity in mixed-grass prairie. *Vegetatio* 64: 87-94.

26. Dale, V.H., S. Brown, R.A. Haeuber, N.T. Hobbs, N. Huntly, R.J. Naiman, W.E. Biebsame, M.G. Turner and T.J. Valone. 2000. Ecological principles and guidelines for managing the use of land. *Ecological Applications* 10(3): 639-670.

27. Doerr, T.B., E.F. Redente, and F.B. Reeves. 1984. Effects of soil disturbance on plant succession and levels of mycorrhizal fungi in a sage-brush-grassland community. *Journal of Range Management* 37(2): 135-139.

28. Donahue, D.L. 1999. *The Western Range Revisited: Removing Livestock from Public Lands to Conserve Native Biodiversity.* Norman: University of Oklahoma Press.

29. Dormaar, J.F., S. Smoliak and W.D. Willms. 1989. Vegetation and soil responses to short-duration grazing on fescue grasslands. *Journal of Range Management* 42(3): 252-256.

30. Dyksterhuis, E.J. 1949. Condition and management of range land based on quantitative ecology. *Journal of Range Management* 2(3): 104-115.

31. Eldridge, D.J. and R. Rosentreter. 1999. Morphological groups: A framework for monitoring microphytic crusts in arid landscapes. *Journal of Arid Environments* 41: 11-25.

32. Elkins, N.Z., G.V. Sabol, T.J. Ward, and W.G. Whitford. 1986. The influence of subterranean termites on the hydrological characteristics of a Chihuahuan desert ecosystem. *Oecologia* 68: 521-528.

33. Elmore, W. and B. Kauffman. 1994. Riparian and watershed systems: Degradation and restoration. *In* Martin Vavra, William A. Laycock and Rex D. Pieper, eds. *Ecological Implications of Livestock Herbivory in the West,* pp. 212-231. Denver: Society for Range Management.

34. Ethridge, D.E., R.D. Sherwood, R.E. Sosebee, and C.H. Herbel. 1997. Economic feasibility of rangeland seeding in the arid southwest. *Journal of Range Management* 50: 185-190.

35. Fredrickson, E., K.M. Havstad, R. Estell and P. Hyder. 1998. Perspectives on desertification: south-western United States. *Journal of Arid*

Environments 39: 191-207.

36. Friedel, M.H. 1991. Range condition assessment and the concept of thresholds: A viewpoint. *Journal of Range Management* 44(5): 422-426.

37. Fuhlendorf, S.D. and F.E. Smeins. 1999. Scaling effects of grazing in a semi-arid grassland. *Journal of Vegetation Science* 10: 731-738.

38. Gamougoun, N.D., R.P. Smith, M.K. Wood and R.D. Pieper. 1984. Soil, vegetation, and hydrologic responses to grazing management at Fort Stanton, New Mexico. *Journal of Range Management* 37(6): 538-541.

39. Gillen, R.L., F.T. McCollum, M.E. Hodges, J.E. Brummer and K.W. Tate. 1991. Plant community responses to short duration grazing in tallgrass prairie. *Journal of Range Management* 44(2): 124-128.

40. Glenn, S.M. and S.L. Collins. 1991. Effects of scale and disturbance on rates of immigration and extinction of species in prairies. *Oikos* 63: 273-280.

41. Goodloe, S. 1969. Short duration grazing in Rhodesia. *Journal of Range Management* 22: 369-373.

42. Grazing Lands Technical Institute. 1997. *National Range and Pasture Handbook.* Washington, D.C.: U.S.D.A., Natural Resources Conservation Service.

43. Griffiths, David. 1904. Range Investigations in Arizona. U.S. Department of Agriculture Bureau of Plant Industry Bulletin No. 67. Washington, D.C.: Government Printing Office.

44. Gutierrez, J.R. and W.G. Whitford. 1987. Chihuahuan desert annuals: Importance of water and nitrogen. *Ecology* 68(6): 2032-2045.

45. Hart, R.H., M.J. Samuel, P.S. Test and M.A. Smith. 1988. Cattle, vegetation, and economic responses to grazing systems and grazing pressure. *Journal of Range Management* 41(4): 282-286.

46. Havstad, K.M. 1999. Improving sustainability of arid rangelands. *New Mexico Journal of Science* 39: 174-197.

47. Havstad, K.M. and D.P. Coffin-Peters. 1999. People and rangeland biodiversity—North America. *In Proceedings of the VIth International Rangeland Congress, Townsville, Australia,* vol. 2, pp. 634-638.

48. Heitschmidt, R.K., D.L. Price, R.A. Gordon and J.R. Frasure. 1982. Short duration grazing at the Texas Experimental Ranch: Effects on aboveground net primary production and seasonal dynamics. *Journal of Range Management* 35(3): 367-372.

49. Heitschmidt, R. and J. Walker. 1983. Short duration grazing and the Savory grazing method in perspective. *Rangelands* 5(4): 147-150.

50. Herbel, C.H., F.N. Ares and R.A. Wright. 1972. Drought effects on a semidesert grassland range. *Ecology* 53(6): 1084-1093.

51. Herbel, C.H. and R.P. Gibbens. 1996. Post-Drought Vegetation Dynamics on Arid Rangelands of Southern New Mexico. New Mexico State University Agricultural Experiment Station Bulletin 776.

52. Hik, D.S. and R.L. Jefferies. 1990. Increases in the net above-ground primary production of a salt-marsh forage grass: A test of the predictions of the herbivore-optimization model. *Journal of Ecology* 78: 180-195.

53. Hobbs, N.T. 1996. Modification of ecosystems by ungulates. *Journal of Wildlife Management* 60(4): 695-712.

54. Hobbs, R.J. and L.F. Huenneke. 1992. Disturbance, diversity, and invasion: Implications for conservation. *Conservation Biology* 6(3): 324-337.

55. Holechek, J.L. and T. Stephenson. 1983. Comparison of big sagebrush vegetation in northcentral New Mexico under moderately grazed and grazing excluded conditions. *Journal of Range Management* 36(4): 455-456.

56. Holechek, J.L., R.D. Pieper, and C.H. Herbel. 1998. *Range Management: Principles and Practices.* Third edition. Upper Saddle River, N.J.: Prentice Hall.

57. Holechek, J. L., H. Gomez, F. Molinar, and D. Galt. 1999. Grazing studies: What we've learned. *Rangelands* 21(2): 12-16.

58. Holechek, J. L., M. Thomas, F. Molinar, and D. Galt. 1999. Stocking desert rangelands: What we've learned. *Rangelands* 21(6): 8-12.

59. Holechek, J.L., H. Gomes, F. Molinar, D. Galt, and R. Valdez. 2000. Short-duration grazing: The facts in 1999. *Rangelands* 22(1): 18-22.

60. Jackson, W. 1998. Agricultural and human communities when nature's prairie is the standard. *In* Tellman, B., D.M. Finch, C. Edminster, R. Hamre, eds. *The Future of Arid Grasslands: Identifying Issues, Seeking Solutions,* pp. 203- 209. 1996 Oct. 9-13; Tucson, AZ. Proceedings. RMRS-P-3. Fort Collins, CO: U.S. Department of Agriculture, Forest Service, Rocky Mountain Research Station.

61. Johansen, J.R. and L.L. St. Clair. 1986. Cryptogamic soil crusts: Recovery from grazing near Camp Floyd State Park, Utah, USA. *Great Basin Naturalist* 46(4): 632-640.

62. Jornada Experimental Range. 2000. *Monitoring Manual for Grassland, Shrubland and Savanna Ecosystems.* Las Cruces: USDA-Agricultural Research Service.

63. Jung, H.G., R.W. Rice and L.J. Koong. 1985. Comparison of heifer weight gains and forage quality for continuous and short-duration grazing systems. *Journal of Range Management* 38(2): 144-148.

64. Kauffman, J.B. and W.C. Krueger. 1984. Livestock impacts on riparian ecosystems and streamside management implications. . .A review. *Journal of Range Management* 37(5): 430-438.

65. Kirby, D.R., M.F. Pessin and G.K. Clambey. 1986. Disappearance of forage under short duration and season-long grazing. *Journal of Range Management* 39(6): 496-500.

66. Laycock, W.A. 1991. Stable states and thresholds of range condition on North American rangelands: A viewpoint. *Journal of Range Management* 44(5): 427-433.

67. Lewis, J.K. 1969. Range management viewed in the ecosystem framework. *In* G.M. Van Dyne, ed. *The Ecosystem concept in Natural Resource Management.* New York: Academic Press.

68. Ludwig, J., D. Tongway, D. Freudenberger, J. Noble, and K. Hodgkinson, eds. 1997. *Landscape Ecology, Function and Management: Principles from Australia's Rangelands.* Collingwood, Australia: CSIRO Publishing.

69. Martin, S.C. 1975. Ecology and Management of Southwestern Semidesert Grass-Shrub Ranges: The Status of Our Knowledge. USDA Forest Service Research Paper RM-156.

70. MacKay, W.P., J.C. Zak, and W.G. Whitford. 1989. The natural history and role of subterranean termites in the northern Chihuahuan desert. *In* J.O. Schmidt, ed. *Special Biotic Relationships in the Arid Southwest,* pp. 53-77. Albuquerque: University of New Mexico Press.

71. McNaughton, S.J. 1979. Grazing as an optimization process: grass-ungulate relationships in the Serengeti. *American Naturalist* 113(5): 691-703.

72. McNaughton, S.J. 1983. Compensatory plant growth as a response to herbivory. *Oikos* 40(3): 329-336.

73. McNaughton, S.J. 1985. Ecology of a grazing ecosystem: The Serengeti. *Ecological Monographs* 55(3): 259-294.

74. McNaughton, S.J. 1986. On plants and herbivores. *American Naturalist* 128(5): 765-770.

75. McPherson, G.R. 1995. The role of fire in the desert grasslands. *In* M.P. McClaran and T.R. Van Devender, eds. *The Desert Grassland,* pp. 130-151. Tucson: University of Arizona Press.

76. McPherson, G.R. and J.F. Weltzin. 2000. Disturbance and Climate Change in United States/Mexico Borderland Plant Communities: A State-of-the-Knowledge Review. Gen. Tech. Rep. RMRS-GTR-50. Fort Collins, CO: U.S. Department of Agriculture, Forest Service, Rocky Mountain Research Station.

77. Milchunas, D.G. and W.K. Lauenroth. 1993. Quantitative effects of grazing on vegetation and soils over a global range of environments. *Ecological Monographs* 63: 327-366.

78. National Research Council. 1994. *Rangeland Health: New Methods to Classify, Inventory, and Monitor Rangelands.* Washington, D.C.: National Academy Press.

79. Oesterheld, M., O.E. Sala and S.J. McNaughton. 1992. Effect of animal husbandry on herbivore-carrying capacity at a regional scale. *Nature* 356: 234-236.

80. Olson, K.C. and J.C. Malechek. 1988. Heifer nutrition and growth on short duration grazed crested wheatgrass. *Journal of Range Management* 41(3): 259-263.

81. Owen, D.F. and R.G. Wiegert. 1981. Mutualism between grasses and grazers: An evolutionary hypothesis. *Oikos* 36(3): 376-378.

82. Paulsen, H.A. Jr. and F.N. Ares. 1962. Grazing Values and Management of Black Grama and Tobosa Grasslands and Associated Shrub Ranges of the Southwest. U.S.D.A. Forest Service Technical Bulletin No. 1270.

83. Pfister, J.A., G.B. Donart, R.D. Pieper, J.D. Wallace and E.E. Parker. 1984. Cattle diets under continuous and four-pasture, one-herd grazing systems in southcentral New Mexico. *Journal of Range Management* 37(1): 50-54.

84. Pieper, R.D. 1980. Impacts of grazing systems on livestock. *In Proceedings: Grazing Management Systems for Southwest Rangelansd Symposium.* April 1-2, 1980, Albuquerque, N.M. Las Cruces: New Mexico State University Range Improvement Task Force.

85. Pieper, R.D. 1994. Ecological implications of livestock grazing. *In* Martin Vavra, William A. Laycock and Rex D. Pieper, eds. *Ecological Implications of Livestock Herbivory in the West,* pp. 177-211. Denver: Society for Range Management.

86. Pieper, R.D. and R.K. Heitschmidt. 1988. Is short-duration grazing the answer? *Journal of Soil and Water Conservation* 43(2): 133-137.

87. Pluhar, J.J., R.W. Knight and R.K. Heitschmidt. 1987. Infiltration rates and sediment production as influenced by grazing systems in the Texas rolling plains. *Journal of Range Management* 40(3): 240-243.

88. Rincon Institute. 1998. *Conservation Options for Landowners: A Guide to the Tools and Benefits of Protecting Natural Areas on Private Land.* Tucson: Rincon Institute.

89. Roundy, B.A. and S.H. Biedenbender. 1995. Revegetation in the desert grassland. *In* M.P. McClaran and T.R. Van Devender, eds. *The Desert Grassland,* pp. 265-304. Tucson: University of Arizona Press.

90. St. Clair, L.L., J.B. Johansen and S.R. Rushforth. 1993. Lichens of soil crust communities in the intermountain area of the western United States. *Great Basin Naturalist* 53(1): 5-12.

91. Sampson, A.W. 1919. Plant Succession in Relation to Range Management. U.S.D.A. Bulletin No. 791. Washington, D.C.: Government Printing Office.

92. Savory, A. 1983. The Savory grazing method or holistic resource management. *Rangelands* 5(4): 155-159.

93. Savory, A. with J. Butterfield. 1999. *Holistic Management: A New Framework for Decision Making.* Washington, D.C.: Island Press.

Bibliography

94. Scarnecchia, D.L. 1999. Viewpoint: The range utilization concept, allocation arrays, and range management science. *Journal of Range Management* 52(2): 157-160.

95. Schlesinger, W.H., J.F. Reynolds, G.L. Cunningham, L.F. Huenneke, W.M. Jarrell, R.A. Virginia and W.G. Whitford. 1990. Biological feedbacks in global desertification. *Science* 247: 1043-1048.

96. Schlesinger, W.H., J.A. Raikes, A.E. Hartley and A.F. Cross. 1996. On the spatial pattern of soil nutrients in desert ecosystems. *Ecology* 77(2): 364-374.

97. Skovlin, J. 1987. Southern Africa's experience with intensive short duration grazing. *Rangelands* 9(4): 162-167.

98. Smith, Jared G. 1899. Grazing Problems in the Southwest and How to Meet Them. U.S. Department of Agriculture Division of Agrostology Bulletin No. 16. Washington, D.C.: Government Printing Office.

99. Sonoran Institute. 1997. *Preserving Working Ranches in the West.* Tucson: Sonoran Institute.

100. Stohlgren, T.J., L.D. Schell and B. Vanden Heuvel. 1999. How grazing and soil quality affect native and exotic plant diversity in Rocky Mountain grasslands. *Ecological Applications* 9(1): 45-64.

101. Svejcar, T. and J.R. Brown. 1992. Is the Range Condition Concept Compatible with Ecosystem Dynamics? Symposium, Annual Meeting of the Society for Range Management, Spokane.

102. Thurow, T.L. n.d. Assessment of brush management as a strategy for enhancing water yield. *At*: http://twri.tamu.edu/twriconf/w4tx98/papers/thurow.html.

103. Thurow, T.L., W.H. Blackburn and C.A. Taylor, Jr. 1986. Hydrologic characteristics of vegetation types as affected by livestock grazing systems, Edwards Plateau, Texas. *Journal of Range Management* 41(4): 296-302.

104. Thurow, T.L., W.H. Blackburn and C.A. Taylor, Jr. 1988a. Infiltration and interrill erosion responses to selected livestock grazing strategies, Edwards Plateau, Texas. *Journal of Range Management* 39(6): 505-509.

105. Thurow, T.L., W.H. Blackburn and C.A. Taylor, Jr. 1988b. Some vegetation responses to selected livestock grazing strategies, Edwards Plateau, Texas. *Journal of Range Management* 41(2): 108-114.

106. Tongway, D.J. and J.A. Ludwig. 1997. The conservation of water and nutrients within landscapes. *In* J. Ludwig, D. Tongway, D. Freudenberger, J. Noble, and K. Hodgkinson, eds. *Landscape Ecology, Function and Management: Principles from Australia's Rangelands,* pp. 13-22. Collingwood, Australia: CSIRO Publishing.

107. Trlica, M.J., M. Buwal and J.W. Menke. 1977. Effects of rest following defoliations on the recovery of several range species. *Journal of Range Management* 30(1): 21-27.

108. Valone, T.J. and D.A. Kelt. 1999. Fire and grazing in a shrub-invaded arid grassland community: Independent or interactive ecological effects? *Journal of Arid Environments* 42: 15-28.

109. Van Poolen, H.W. and J.R. Lacey. 1979. Herbage response to grazing systems and stocking intensities. *Journal of Range Management* 32(4): 250-253.

110. Vavra, M., W.A. Laycock, and R.D. Pieper. 1994. *Ecological Implications of Livestock Herbivory in the West.* Denver: Society for Range Management.

111. Walker, J.W., R.K. Heitschmidt, E.A. De Morales, M.M. Kothmann and S.L. Dowhower. 1989. Quality and botanical composition of cattle diets under rotational and continuous grazing treatments. *Journal of Range Management* 42(3): 239-242.

112. Warren, S.D., W.H. Blackburn and C.A. Taylor, Jr. 1986a. Effects of season and stage of rotation cycle on hydrologic condition of rangeland under intensive rotation grazing. *Journal of Range Management* 39(6): 486-491.

113. Warren, S.D., W.H. Blackburn and C.A. Taylor, Jr. 1986b. Soil hydrologic response to number of pastures and stocking density under intensive rotation grazing. *Journal of Range Management* 39(6): 500-504.

114. Warren, S.D., T.L. Thurow, W.H. Blackburn and N.E. Garza. 1986. The influence of livestock trampling under intensive rotation grazing on soil hydrologic characteristics. *Journal of Range Management* 39(6): 491-495.

115. Weltz, M. and M.K. Wood. 1986. Short duration grazing in central New Mexico: Effects on infiltration rates. *Journal of Range Management* 39(4): 365-368.

116. West, N.E., F.D. Provenza, P.S. Johnson, and M.K. Owens. 1984. Vegetation change after 13 years of livestock exclusion on sagebrush semi-desert in west central Utah. *Journal of Range Management* 37(3): 262-264

117. Westoby, M., B. Walker and I. Noy-Meir. 1989. Opportunistic management for rangelands not at equilibrium. *Journal of Range Management* 42(4): 266-274.

118. Whalley, R.D.B. 1994. State and transition models for rangelands. 1. Successional theory and vegetation change. *Tropical Grasslands* 28: 195-205.

119. Whitford, W.G. 1996. The importance of the biodiversity of soil biota in arid ecosystems. *Biodiversity and Conservation* 5: 185-195.

120. Whitford, W.G. 2000. Keystone arthropods as webmasters in desert ecosystems. *In* D.C. Coleman and P.F. Hendrix, eds. *Invertebrates as*

Webmasters in Ecosystems, pp. 25-41. CAB International.

    121. Whitford, W.G., G.S. Forbes, and G.I. Kerley. 1995. Diversity, spatial variability, and functional roles of invertebrates in desert grassland ecosystems. *In* M.P. McClaran and T.R. Van Devender, eds. *The Desert Grassland,* pp. 152-195. Tucson: University of Arizona Press.

    122. Whitford, W.G. and J.E. Herrick. 1995. Maintaining soil processes for plant productivity and community. *Fifth International Rangeland Congress Proceedings,* pp.33-37.

    123. Winder, J.A., C.C. Bailey, M. Thomas, and J. Holechek. 2000. Breed and stocking rate effects on Chihuahuan Desert cattle production. *Journal of Range Management* 53: 32-38.

    124. Wooten, E.O. 1908. The Range Problem in New Mexico. New Mexico Agricultural Experiment Station Bulletin No. 66.

Quotation Cites

Table of Contents, p. iii
> Speech by James Ingalls, U.S. Senator from Kansas, 1873-1891.

Preface, p. viii
> *A Sand County Almanac* (1949). Aldo Leopold.

Chapter One, p. 9
> See # 60 above.

Chapter Two, p. 21
> *American Places* (1981). Wallace Stegner.

Chapter Three, p. 35
> Poem, quoted in *Japan Environment Monitor*, No. 1, April 30, 1991. Makoto Ooka.

Chapter Four, p. 48
> *Silent Spring* (1962). Rachel Carson.

Chapter Five, p. 62
> *What Are People For?* (1990). Wendell Berry.

Chapter Six, p. 77
> *What Are People For?* (1990). Wendell Berry.

Conclusion, p. 87
> *The Sound of Mountain Water* (1969). Wallace Stegner.

Bibliography, p. 92
> *Annajanska* (1919). George Bernard Shaw.

(Photo courtesy of Courtney White.)

About the Author

Nathan Sayre holds a Ph.D. in Anthropology from the University of Chicago, and is presently a post-doctoral researcher with the Agricultural Research Service—Jornada Experimental Range. He has been studying ranching, conservation, and urbanization issues in the Southwest for the past five years, and has worked extensively with the Quivira Coalition, the Altar Valley Conservation Alliance, and the Pima County-Sonoran Desert Conservation Plan's Ranch Conservation Technical Advisory Team.

Nathan's doctoral dissertation, on the Buenos Aires Ranch and its transformation into a National Wildlife Refuge, will be published by University of Arizona Press under the title *Species of Capital: Ranching, Endangered Species, and Urbanization in the Southwest*. He lives in Tucson with his wife Lucia and his son, Henry (pictured above with the author).